Documents in Canadian Architecture

Patkau Architects

Tuns Press
Faculty of Architecture
Dalhousie University
P.O. Box 1000
Halifax, Nova Scotia
Canada B3J 2X4
URL: www.dal.ca/tunspress

General Editor: Essy Baniassad
Manager: Donald Westin

Distributed in the United Kingdom and Europe by:
Cardiff Academic Press, St. Fagans Road,
Fairwater, Cardiff CF5 3AE, United Kingdom

Patkau Architects: Selected Projects 1983-1993
Editor: Brian Carter
Design: George Vaitkunas, Michael Kothke, John Patkau, Patricia Patkau
Production: Donald Westin
Printing: Atlantic Nova Print Co.

Canadian Cataloguing in Publication Data
Patkau Architects
        (Documents in Canadian Architecture)
        ISBN 0-929112-28-8
1. Patkau Architects (Firm) 2. Architecture, Modern – 20th century –
British Columbia – Designs and plans. I. Carter, Brian. II. Patkau
Architects (Firm). III. Series.

NA749.P38A4 1994   720'.92711   C94-950012-7

Acknowledgments

Preparing this Monograph has involved a number of people without whose cooperation and support it would not have been possible. My thanks are first and foremost to Essy Baniassad for welcoming the idea of a series of Monographs on Canadian architecture and enthusiastically supporting the preparation of this first publication in that series with his boundless energy, good advice, incisive criticism and generous commitment of resources. Given that encouragement to make a start and to carry on to the finish, particular thanks must go to John and Patricia Patkau and their colleagues in the office for their special help, enthusiasm, unflagging energy and patience, firstly in designing buildings which so inspired, and then in creating much of the raw material for this publication. The hard work and inspiration of Donald Westin of TUNS Press in Halifax and the advice and efforts of George Vaitkunas and Michael Kothke in Vancouver were invaluable in realizing the design and production of the book. Thanks must also go to Kenneth Frampton, to Bronwen Ledger and Beth Kapusta of The Canadian Architect and Marco Polo in Toronto for their generous contributions, as well as to Grant Wanzel and Annette W. LeCuyer who both created space, time and quiet for me to work in Halifax and Greenwich.

Through the cooperation of Constance Barrett, Bob Allies and Graham Morrison of the Exhibitions Committee of the Royal Institute of British Architects in London, and of Fiona McLoughlan and Martin Berkhans in Edinburgh it was possible to plan the publication of this Monograph to coincide with an exhibition of the Patkaus' work undertaken with the assistance of the Government of Canada with the particular support of Michael Regan in London.

The publication of this Monograph has been made possible with financial support made available through the efforts of the UK/Canada Architecture Group under the direction of its chairman Martin Berkhans and Michael J. Hellyer, the Academic Affairs Officer of the Canadian High Commission in London, and the unfailing assistance, enthusiasm and resources of the School of Architecture of the Technical University of Nova Scotia.

B.C.

Foreword
Dr. E. Baniassad

Architecture in Canada combines the richness of Western architectural heritage and the simplicity of an aboriginal culture still closely tied to a vast fragile land. Except within the thin "civilized" zone at its extreme south, coping with the bare essentials of daily life is the lot of Canada's people. Within Canada's culture, there exists a duality of cultivated sophistication rooted in Western culture and a primitive simplicity derived from its original people. Canada's architecture derives an urbane quality from its European heritage which makes it appear to be an integral extension of that heritage, but Canada's North has another rich heritage, with its own history, mythology, formal innocence and poetic freshness.

The best of Canadian architecture displays the search for a resolution of this duality, a resolution which is just as difficult to identify and name in specific instances as would be a "distinctive" Canadian architecture. Such an architecture embraces the European tradition, with its well developed language and grammar, shyly. In its most poetic works this architecture reflects a search for a less assertive and gentle reflection of the mythology and aesthetics of the Inuit and other Canadian natives.

This architecture is not merely a body of works which adds to the general volume of Western architecture. It also has an illusive and importantly original quality which is more than merely a colonial extension and elaboration of European models. This original quality is similar to that which Northrop Frye once

identified in Canadian poetry, that is, the quality of primitive simplicity that keeps eluding the poets of a more complex society, however earnestly they seek it. ("Expanding Eye," *Spiritus Mundi*, p.121)

The most effective way to identify, define, and establish the content and the scope of these contributions is to document leading examples of them. That is the objective behind this and upcoming publications of the present series — *Documents in Canadian Architecture*.

The work of Patkau Architects is an excellent example of the search for the resolution of the Canadian cultural duality. It may not be the most voluminous, or perhaps the most refined, but it is certainly amongst the most searching and poetic architecture of our time. Patkau's work skillfully avoids extra-architectural aims. Their attitude is that they practice architecture like any other architect, not setting out to create "Canadian Architecture," but simply architecture.

The architecture of the Patkaus is the subject of the first volume in this series of publications. The aim is to produce documents that offer an insight into the process of design by documenting the "facts" and the products of the process: the sketches, drawings, and the end products. The documents in this series include not only pictures of end products, but also pictures and drawings made from the point of view of the design architect for purposes of the study of architecture. Hopefully this series is free from the publicizing and advertising tendency that so often haunts such publications. As a series, *Documents in Canadian*

Architecture aims to present architectural work as clearly and directly as possible, in a way that is unobscured by unnecessary rhetoric or biased presentation.

In this series, confidence in the quality of the work will reinforce the importance of exposing it to critical examination. My hope is that this publication will be an initial offering to the critical study of its subject.

December 1993

Foreword to the Second Edition

I am pleased that as a result of appreciative and enthusiastic response to the original edition of this book it has become necessary so soon after its first publication to go ahead with a second edition. The original edition has been kept the same except in a few points of composition and layout. The response to the publication of this book on the work of Pat and John Patkau is not only a clear sign of the significance of their work, it is also a sign of the wide interest in architecture. The original publication has already received insightful and constructive critical comments from many colleagues and critics. These are important contributions to our effort and it is with regret that the current edition does not offer the opportunity to reflect these comments. Amongst these I would like particularly to acknowledge the encouragement of Andrew Gruft whose own work in exhibitions and publications have shown early and fine examples for studies of architecture in Canada.

July 1994

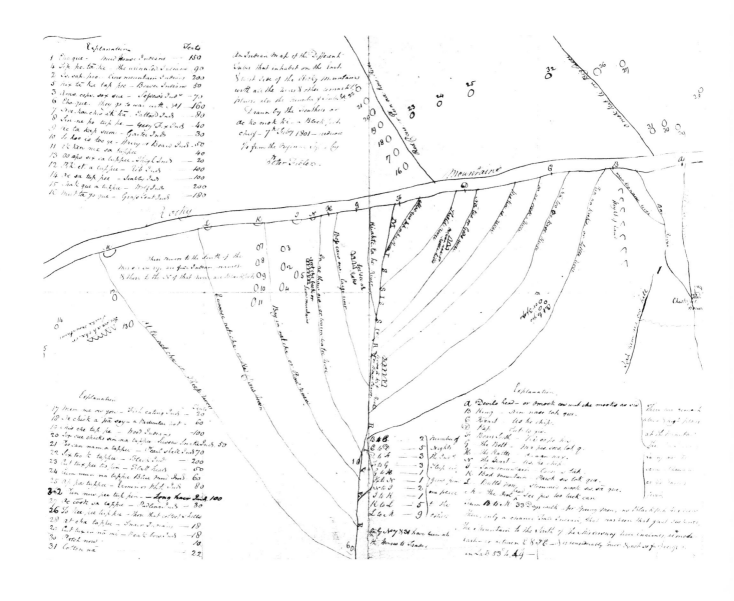

Mapping Territory
Brian Carter

"The Hudson Bay Company, like many other companies, depended on Indians for geographical information.... From the earliest contact until the recent past, Europeans solicited information about unexplored and superficially explored areas. The Indians responded, communicating geographical information in a mixture of speech, gesture and pictography. Pictographs, usually in the form of 'maps', were particularly important in influencing the structure and content of maps drawn by Europeans." [1]

The mapping of the land, realized by tenacious exploration, the precision of the survey and the vivid observations of the native was fundamental in establishing a description of Canada. The work of John and Patricia Patkau can be interpreted as an effort to map an architectural ground which reflects those same preoccupations with discovery and invention.

Working first along the wide horizon of the Prairies and more recently at the coastal edge of the Pacific North West these two young Canadian architects have made their explorations through the rigours of practice.

They have created an architecture which seems to be deeply rooted in their particular territory; the expansive, dramatic and largely uninhabited landscapes, the stubborn attitude of a people committed to survival and the effort to build a new country. Although the projects they have designed — a mix of private houses and public buildings — have been small, their significance is considerable.

Most of these houses are beyond the city, sometimes remote and usually within areas of outstanding natural beauty that are often hidden deep within the forest or close to the ocean. In sharp contrast to the long established and densely built landscapes of Europe which are marked by ancient ley lines, boundaries and layers of history, these buildings frequently represent the first acts of settlement. It is this taking up of the land which has been a fundamental influence in the development of the architecture of the Patkaus.

As if to encourage survival in these rugged places their rigorous scrutiny and mapping of the landscape and its terra firma has, like the attention of wise travellers, sought to reveal appropriate places to settle. However, this is a discovery of site which has informed their plans to build without resorting to primitivism or an earthy mysticism. In a manner which recalls the inspiration of Aalto their houses have become an extension of the ground in a way which often makes it difficult to distinguish between building and site. So in the organization of its plan, the Patkaus' own house in West Vancouver first forms a low retaining wall that hints at a path on the mountain — a path which then weaves its way down the steep wooded slope and through the house to a watercourse drumming along the valley below. Rooms within the house, articulated in section and defined with light, are conspicuously opened to the path and the forest beyond.

"An Indian Map of the Different Tribes that inhabit on the East & West Side of the Rocky Mountains with all the rivers & other remarkbl. places, also the Number of Tents etc. Drawn by the Feathers or Ac ko mok ki — a Black foot chief — 7th Feby. 1801 — reduced 1/4 from the Original Size — by Peter Fidler." HBCA Map Collection, G.1/25 (N4157) Hudson's Bay Company Archives, Provincial Archives of Manitoba

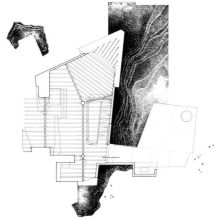

In Nanaimo, the compacted boulder-like form of the recently completed Barnes House has been wedged into a crack in the mountain whilst at the Pyrch House rooms are strung out in an informal line which has been cranked to form three sides of a courtyard containing talismanic fragments of the rock of the site. Two tall post-like chimneys stake out the extremities of that courtyard and at the same time frame a view to the distant ocean.

The planning of most of these houses, like the Patkaus' drawings, maintains a simple diagrammatic quality whilst the construction of the envelope utilizes common materials and techniques — the ubiquitous stud frame clad in drywall — to create a series of singular isolated objects which are reliant only on themselves for authenticity. Although the house is the most fundamental of types the design of these particular projects demonstrates an attempt to efface the traces of the familiar imagery of idealized forms. Instead a series of elemental pieces, designed and selected to recall the most basic fundamentals of habitation, have been strategically placed on the site and within the relatively neutral fields defined by the plans. So the two chimney posts which mark out the territory of the Pyrch House also hint at the fires of primitive hearths whilst a single freestanding monumental bracketed column located at the heart of the Appleton Residence

refers to earth, air, and sky in a manner that suggests the first act of shelter and the primitive hut. These discoveries of site and the invention of ways of occupying it reflect a preoccupation with grounding — an approach when, according to Heidegger, a site and the siting of something does not exist prior to the idea of that which is to be sited.

Two projects prompted consideration of these preoccupations beyond the private realm of the house to connect with ideas of the nature of civic building in the late twentieth century. One was a school and the other a gallery. The proposal prepared by Patkau Architects for an invited national competition to design the Canadian Clay and Glass Gallery was submitted in 1986. The selection of their scheme from a group of eight submissions however proved premature and as a result of budgetary constraints the project was shelved, albeit temporarily, whilst funding was secured. By the time that work on this scheme was restarted they had also developed the design of the other project. In 1988, the Patkaus were commissioned by the Seabird Island Band to design a new school for the Salish people on a site at Agassiz in the Fraser Valley. Under a new initiative, and with the advice of the Department of Indian Affairs and Northern Development under the direction of Marie-Odile Marceau, the Regional Architect of DIAND in Vancouver, they worked directly with the members of that community to develop a design for a new building which

not only appropriately reflected their specific wants and needs but one that they could also construct themselves.

The zoomorphic form which was developed for the school, with a great folding roof providing protection from the severe winter winds from the north and opening up to the existing village on the south side, was unpredictable. The design, which was derived from a set of surprisingly complex geometries, presented an equivalent complexity in its construction. Seabird Island School, meticulously detailed and extremely well built, represents a significant transition in the development of the work of the Patkaus. Marked by a confrontation with the design and construction of a radically different building type this project was realized with the help of the speech, gestures and pictography of a First Nations community. It also coincided with Patricia Patkau's appointment to the faculty of the University of California at Los Angeles and the Patkaus direct experience of the work of architects like Thomas Mayne and Michael Rotundi. The effects of this transition are detectable in the development of the design for the Clay and Glass Gallery. Whilst the original competition submission drawings show a scheme rooted in the language of earlier houses — smooth soffits concealing constructional framing, a uniformity in the thinness of the wall and the formation of the openings together with a diagrammatic

description of structure perhaps best summarized by those drawings showing the brackets which were to support the external canopy — the subsequent design indicates a more highly developed concern for type, materiality and tectonic detail framed within the context of a systemic view of construction.

The consequence of this move towards an architecture of isolation inspired not only by the characteristics of the site but also by a reconsideration of type and the detail of its construction is clearly evident in the design and realization of both the Clay and Glass Gallery and the new Library at Newton which was designed two years later. Each develops a highly original view about the nature of an established historical model. The Gallery, with its simple shed-like volumes constructed from a limited palette of materials which are clearly expressed and assembled in an obvious manner, has become an industrial place. Embodying a spirit derived from the nature of this particular collection the building, like the spaces created by the artist Donald Judd for the Chinati Foundation in Texas or the Archaeological Museum at Merida designed by Rafael Moneo, expresses a view of the Gallery not as an elaborate temple of culture or the storehouse for art but as a place of work, fabrication and discovery. The public library at Newton — a new suburb on the forested edge of Vancouver — also adopts the form of the shed. Like the Gallery this design also develops a range of conditions of varying complexity and thickness at the line of the wall but here

explores its potential together with that of a structural frame to create the sense of a light, open shelter placed in a man-made clearing and designed to be readily accessible to the families of the fast growing suburb.

The recently completed Barnes House — a residential project with an intricate canopy of timber contained within dense walls, supported on carefully detailed concrete columns with steel brackets and extended with a projecting metal visor — represents perhaps their most distinct departure from the earlier drywalled houses and also embodies many of these other developing ideas. It has been followed by further commissions to design two new educational buildings. Strawberry Vale School will provide facilities for children focussed around a path which meanders down a rocky hillside in Victoria, whilst Patkau's design for new art school spaces for Emily Carr College which is currently under construction on Granville Island in the heart of the city of Vancouver investigates distinctions between public and private domaines in an intensely urban setting. These are projects which place the Patkaus in a new territory — a territory which provides for the discovery of fundamentally different sites as well as the invention of both type and construction.

---

[1] Introduction from the catalogue of the exhibition "Taking up the land: The mapping of Canada through four centuries", mounted at Canada House in London from July 22 - September 25, 1992.

Conversations with Patkau Architects

based on a series of discussions
with Marco Polo, Bronwen Ledger and Beth Kapusta[1]

Could you explain something about the theoretical basis of your work?

Unlike many architects today who are interested in theoretical issues, we did not begin our work in an academic context — we began in the context of practice.

Our development has been marked by the demands of our situation, especially during our early days in Alberta. With only a few years of office experience between us and no examination requirements for professional registration, we embarked upon independent practice. The work of this period was largely conventional. It was a struggle to simply deal with *commodity* and *firmness*, let alone *delight*. We have progressed slowly from this beginning, to develop a theoretical basis for our work that makes sense in terms of the day to day exigencies of practice, as well as the larger world of cultural ideas.

Our present position begins with the observation that people and cultures are defined by the balance that they make between the general and the particular. We feel that in western society this balance is in jeopardy. Mass culture is becoming so predominant that the local and the particular are becoming less and less evident. This is the 'McDonald's theorem' — the proposition that international capitalism is creating a uniform world culture. Architecture can play an important role in this context, as a counterbalance to the increasing generality of other aspects of culture. That is

why we think architecture should become increasingly oriented towards the particular. Of all the arts, architecture is most capable of dealing with the particulars of situation — with 'place'.

One of the recent texts that we have found especially useful is Michael Benedict's book *For an Architecture of Reality*. Among other things, he deals with certain media-related issues and discusses architecture's inability to compete on its own terms with the 'media'. We can't entertain the way movies entertain for example. The argument is that we shouldn't even be attempting to do that — that architecture can do other things and has a different role to play in our lives.

What are the formal or the spatial implications of this in your work?

We begin every project by searching for what we call 'found potential'. Found potential can exist in any aspect of a project. It can be the site, and for us because we have been practising in British Columbia, topography is a conspicuous influence. Climate is also important, especially in terms of light. Program, building context, local culture, the nature of the client — all of these are sources we use to develop an architectural order which is specific to circumstance. In purely formal terms we attempt to achieve particularization and specificity through differentiation. To this end,

[1] The compilation of interviews appears courtesy of Marco Polo, published in *The Toronto Society of Architects' Newsletter*, Spring 1991; Bronwen Ledger and Beth Kapusta, published in *The Canadian Architect*, May 1993.

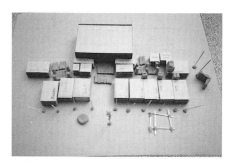

our buildings often utilize devices such as juxtaposition — contrasting scales, or playing mass against void or line, for example. Increasingly, we also tend to differentiate elements within building assemblies, expressing the role of each element, either directly or through representation, so that the nature of the construction and the forces which act upon it are evident.

Can you explain the evolution of the Seabird Island School?

Because the school is for a Native client whose culture is private on many important levels, the building is, at best, an interpretation of that culture.
Our first perception of the project developed upon visiting the site. The space of the island — a flat delta of agricultural land surrounded by mountains — seemed very much like a great room. We felt that the building which was to inhabit this room should have an animated personality, something that could be perceived on a naive level as a 'being' of some kind. We didn't intend that the building represent anything specific. We simply gave it a configuration which would lend itself to interpretation. The members of the band have responded very positively to this aspect of the design. They see things in it that are meaningful to them. A class of architecture students was there on a field trip one day and as they were leaving the site they were stopped by a member of the band who wanted to know what they were

doing. They explained that they had visited the school. The band member said to them " Well you know that it's a salmon" — he was quite convinced that it was a salmon.

The section certainly has a 'fishy' quality about it and can easily be interpreted in that way.

Yes, but we were very careful not to succumb to that way of seeing it. We always viewed it as an abstract construction which, if related to anything in architectural history, is related to German Expressionism not to some North American phenomenon.

It seems to do a number of different things; it does have that biomorphic expression and at the same time the hard angularity which to some extent must be mitigated by its materials.

The shingles which cover the whole building wrap it with a scalelike skin.

How did the project evolve?

The project was a fairly straightforward response to a number of considerations. On an urban level, the school was sited to complete the northern edge of an emerging village square. Classrooms were oriented along the resulting public face of the building, defined by a large porch element. The gym was located behind, providing shelter from the winter winds, with the kindergarten on the east for

Blunden Harbour, 1901, by C.S. Newcombe

morning light. The library and staff facilities took up the resulting interstitial zone.

In terms of massing, we started simply with a lump that represented the large volume required for the gym and a bar that represented the smaller volume of the classrooms. The disjunction between these elements is an issue that plagues most schools. It's always difficult to reconcile their competing masses. We did a lot of models, maybe 20 in the process, each one being an incremental step toward the next. In each model the configuration was manipulated and made more continuous. At the same time, the structure was rationalized.

What about the porch?

We had looked at the traditional building forms of coastal bands. They had some amazing urban architecture organized along boardwalks. The porch comes from that tradition. The idea was that the porch would become the edge of the village square, with gardens and play structures that would be clipped on — vaguely reminiscent of some of the Archigram ideas of structure and clip-on. There was to be a salmon drying rack, which is an ongoing part of their subsistence, as are the gardens, and so we wanted these things to really tie into the way the band lived. In this way the educational experience could be integrated more fully into the life of the community.

The architecture which results from this thinking is quite different from your earlier work. This seems less object- like.

Perhaps that's simply a reflection of the change from 'private' to 'public' projects?
The porch elements here become totemic. They have a representational aspect to them which, incidentally, is not that different from the sunshades on the Kustin house. The Clay and Glass Gallery has a similar totemic arcade. We think these devices are manifestations of a changing spatial sensibility.

Why is that happening?

Our early work in Alberta was spatially and formally homogeneous. Whatever order existed was consistent throughout and although there was richness within that order, the quality and the character of the spaces was similar from one end to the other. This approach was antithetical to place-making.
On the other hand, the Clay and Glass Gallery has an irregularly, or unevenly developed plan, with concentrations of energy in a fairly neutral field.

It seems that this was happening in some of the early projects too. I'm thinking of the Appleton House.

Yes, Appleton is a manifestation of that.

And was that very conscious in Appleton?

No. Appleton was a response to other things. It was a response to a desire for 'substance' in a world made of wood studs and drywall. To achieve this, we created a couple of figures that had density and spatial presence, and placed them within a generally undeveloped plan. The idea being that these figures, principally the column and the fireplace, would act to give the whole house a feeling of substance.
This was done prior to the competition for the Gallery and was the seed of the strategy for our entry. This strategy was centered on the idea of totemic elements; figures which act to place the spectator and artifact in a specific, intensified architectural relationship.

The Canadian Clay and Glass Gallery has changed a lot since the original competition scheme.

When we won the competition there was some question as to whether we would be able to build the building for the budget, and it was quite clear two years later, when the project went ahead, that we couldn't. So we had to radically reduce the scope of the project. One of the major program components eliminated was the glassblowing studio, which was the source of one of the central ideas in the project: that the whole process from making, to collecting, to displaying of art would be made evident, so that people who were in the building could understand it. We wanted it to be clear that there were agencies involved, validating work, putting it on a pedestal and saying "This is good work and trash all this other stuff." We wanted this process to become evident in the building.
When we lost the glassblowing studio, this central idea was destroyed and so we had to reconceive the organization of the building. The revised project addresses the issue of institutionalized culture in a different way. It attempts to connect art to everyday life. In contrast to the neutral white space of the conventional modern gallery, the interior spaces of the Clay and Glass Gallery are very tectonic, all of the construction elements are revealed. It was important to us that art be understood in a context.

Was there resistance to the building being too powerful and taking away from the display of the artifacts?

Yes, there was a lot of concern about that. And legitimately — it is a real issue. But the scale of the architecture versus the scale of the exhibits shown is so dissimilar that it doesn't happen. In actual fact, you can perceive craft and art on the scale of the artifacts and on the scale of the building in a complementary way as opposed to a competitive one.

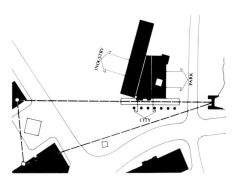

What is the construction?

It is reinforced concrete masonry with brick veneer, steel framing for all the floors and roofs with wood floor deck or roof deck. There is an obvious hierarchy of materials. Wood sits on steel which sits on masonry. It's really straight-forward and that's part of the whole idea of explaining the craft of the building. This is a gallery for highly crafted art and so the whole issue of craft is very significant.

What are the wall finishes?

Concrete block. We feel that the texture and the brutality of block creates a powerful juxta-position to the fragile, delicate character of glass and clay.

The siting of the gallery is interesting relative to the other projects. It is much more urban. What is the siting strategy for this building?

Siting is one of the key issues in all of our projects. But this project, unlike all of the other projects, did not have a 'site'. Most of our other projects have very strong, evident sites. It's interesting that many of the competition entries from Ontario were based on some important relationship to the lake. Coming from British Columbia we didn't perceive this lake, a small pond really, as a powerful element. Instead, we decided to create a site. We started with Barton Myers' pyramid of barrels at the Seagram Museum and then added a water device to celebrate the

point where Silver Lake disappears below grade into a culvert. Our project was then organized as a response to the axis created by these two elements.

How did you feel about being across the street from another museum?

That was very important. We thought it was really an enormous advantage to have another museum there. Our project, with the Seagram Museum, begins to define a cultural precinct, a place in Waterloo which would be comple-mentary to the civic square that was being created beside the new Waterloo City Hall on the other side of the downtown. So to us it was important and fortuitous that Seagram was there.
The intention was to try to make something happen in the long term, the way we imagine Italian piazzas were developed over many decades. Our site strategy was to initiate some form of new world piazza. Time will tell if this is possible.

The interior of the Clay and Glass Gallery is very finely articulated and the mass seems to belie that. There is, perhaps not a schizophrenic relationship but a much more intense concentration of the elaboration of the building internally than externally.

This is a result of the particular technologies involved in the building — and also the climate. Barton Myers published an essay in

The Canadian Architect in November 1977 where he talked about the impact of the severity of the Canadian climate on building configuration: how you have to make simple boxes and then do all the fun stuff inside. There is a lot of merit in this argument and it's reflected in the Clay and Glass Gallery. We should add that we view the Canadian climate as different to the climate of British Columbia so here we do all sorts of things that we would never think of doing in other parts of the country. As a result the buildings here tend to be exteriorized more.

Does that mean you accept the idea of regionalism in architecture?

We are sympathetic to the argument regarding "critical regionalism" outlined by Kenneth Frampton. However we do not believe that the 'regional' is literally the scale within which our projects are conceived. We believe we are working within both an international and a local context. These are the contexts of our architectural decisions.

What about a local school?

Although we are not opposed to the idea, we do not feel we are part of a local school. Nevertheless, there is an expressiveness generally in West Coast architecture, both in the U.S. and Canada, which is distinct from other parts of North America.

We feel that the Barnes house represents what we're trying to do more than what was accomplished with Seabird School. Seabird is too resolved formally for our taste. It's too legible, too clear a composition and we wish that it was more ambiguous and less immediately comprehensible. The Barnes house is a more ambiguous, more irregular object, and that's where our work is heading.

In someone like Aalto's work irregularity would have a lot to do with perspective and the perception of the thing as an object. But what seems really interesting in the Barnes House is that it is much more spatial: the volumetric expression of the building is more important than the object expression.

That's true. Even though our buildings often have strong massing characteristics, the predominant emphasis has always been a spatial one. Those qualities are often difficult to represent in drawings or models or photographs, which is why certain buildings we like more than others, are less successful in terms of their media dimension. They are more difficult to represent. The Appleton house in Victoria, for example, has a very interesting space and that's all it has. But you can't get a good photograph of it so it is not a well-known project.

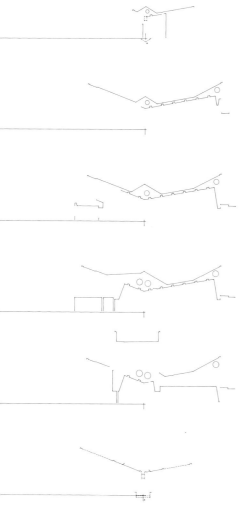

Is that how the design process works? Does it start very much as a spatial conception?

It's more complex than that. It tries to deal with a whole range of things more or less simultaneously. How they come together we're not entirely sure. But a major factor is always the spatial one. If we have a criticism of a lot of work today it is that it tends to be more graphic than spatial. We believe that this is a result of the role photography and the print media have played in warping architecture.

You have talked about Aalto as one of your inspirations in that he was a modernist but he went beyond abstraction.

As students we were extremely interested in Wright, and then Le Corbusier, followed by Aalto. We have taken a close look at many architects and tried to learn as much as we could from each of them. But there isn't any single figure that would be conspicuous as a source of inspiration.
Although Aalto was interested in many of the issues of modernism such as industrialization and the repetition of units, he was also non-modern in many respects. The areas which we find most interesting have to do with the heterogeneity of his work. He tended to use great variety, both spatially and in terms of the elements and materials in his buildings. That offers a tremendously rich palette, capable of adjusting to all sorts of circumstances. We also like his willingness to deal with the fact that buildings sit in the dirt and that buildings get

rained on — all those kinds of nitty-gritty issues. He turned them into art; he made building construction poetic. He took flashings, and copings, and base courses — all the things which the other moderns tried to suppress to allow them to develop an abstract expression — and turned them from necessity into poetry. That's the aspect of Aalto which inspires us.

Many people would say that there is a certain poetry in your work. Do you think there is?

It's something we work hard to achieve. We attempt to define our buildings in poetic terms, but not directly. We try to consider all aspects of a project, becoming more inclusive and expressive as we gain experience and skill. Out of this diversity we hope a subtle and complex poetry can arise — a poetry that is quiet enough and ambiguous enough to be meaningful to others on their own terms.

In terms of an evolution of your work, at what stage is it now?

The work is only at the beginning of the issues of heterogeneity that we are interested in — the variety, the difference and differentiation, the irregularity juxtaposed to regularity. Our work has been predominantly monolithic in the past. Even though it might be an unusual con-figuration like Seabird it is still of a monolithic order throughout. That is something we want to leave behind. We want the buildings to become more differentiated, more irregular, more various.

Selected Projects 1983-1993

Pyrch House
Victoria, British Columbia
1983

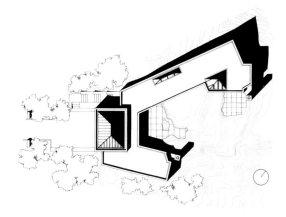

A 232 square meter house for a retired couple who have an excellent collection of non-figurative art. This collection , which includes paintings, works on paper and sculpture, was to be located throughout the house.

Site
Located at a high point in Rockland, an old neighbourhood of very large houses dating from the 1890s, the lot is an irregularly shaped mound of rock, with a frontage of only 10 meters, "left over" in the subdivision of a large estate. There is a beautiful distant view of the ocean to the east. Unfortunately, due to the subdivision development, the immediate overlook of the site in this direction is of a number of newly built "spec" houses of indifferent quality.

Intention
Given the undesirable visual characteristics of the neighbouring houses it was decided that the site should be developed in such a way that the immediate context would be screened without losing the distant view of the ocean. The aesthetic predilection of the client for the abstract, combined with the bold scale of the primordial rock of the site, suggested that the massing of the house, while remaining domestic in scale, should be restricted to a few elemental gestures.
The display of paintings placed a premium on large areas of unbroken wall space so that the amount of window area was necessarily limited. In a climate which is frequently overcast this meant that windows and skylights must be carefully designed and located to maximize the luminosity within the house.

Design
The essential character of the house was established in a single stroke by siting the dominant volume of the house, the living room, to the west, below the peak of the rock mound. In so doing, the immediate context of neighbouring houses to the east was screened, while the distant view of the ocean was framed as a fragment of some perfect landscape, defining a highly abstract terrace of rock and sky.
Once the living room was located, the other spaces of the house were simply wrapped around the adjacent sides of the terrace, with ancillary spaces filling in the low areas of the site below the main level (the garage and service rooms below the living room area and the guest suite below the den area).
The physical dimension of the site (the house is to the setback limit on three sides) in conjunction with our site planning objectives made a regular plan impossible. Yet, given the almost ad hoc connection of room to room en filade we have tried to make each room feel regular in itself so that an aura of reflective calm characterizes the house.
The massing of the house was intended to reinforce the basic organization of the plan and its relationship to the site: A constant parapet line was established against which the highly

variable contours of the site can be clearly measured. Surmounting this constant reference line the dominant volume of the living room was raised in the form of a "chisel-pointed" copper roof. Two largely disengaged chimneys counterbalance the volume of the living room roof. At the same time, these chimneys terminate the mass of the house and mark the distant view of the ocean beyond the terrace. To maximize the luminosity within the house, while maintaining a limited amount of window area, light has been introduced from skylight sources in critical locations. More importantly, however, the windows, themselves, have been designed in conjunction with a variety of millwork items such as bookcases, china and clothing storage, or simply deep casements so that the quality of light coming through the windows is amplified by the reflected light of the adjacent surfaces. In addition, all finishes and colours which receive this light have been selected to enhance the ambient luminosity of the house.

Construction

The house is constructed of conventional stud framing which bears, via a reinforced concrete strip footing, directly upon the exposed rock of the site. The exterior wall finish is pink-grey stucco. Window frames are clear anodized aluminum. The roof over the living room is copper allowed to achieve the luminous green characteristic of the area. Interior wall and ceilings are gypsum board painted white. All millwork is painted white. Floors are bleached oak.

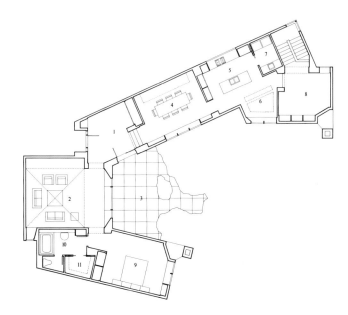

1 entry hall
2 living room
3 terrace
4 dining room
5 kitchen
6 breakfast nook
8 den
9 master bedroom
10 master bath
11 closet
12 guest suite
13 bedroom
14 bathroom

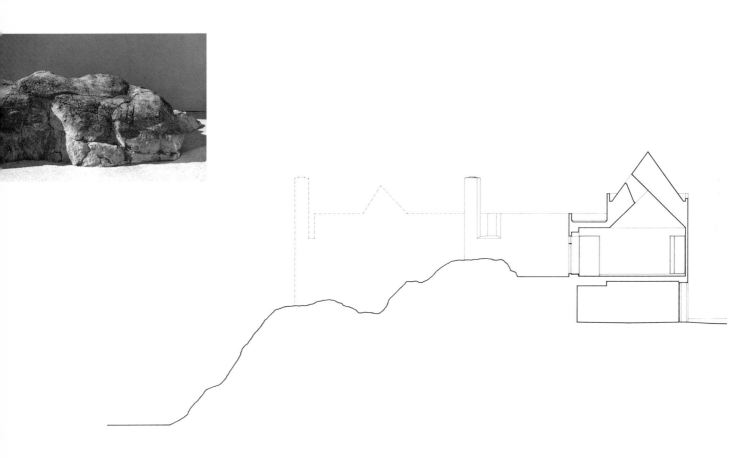

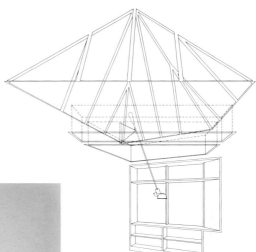

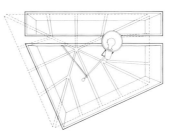

Patkau House
West Vancouver, British Columbia
1984

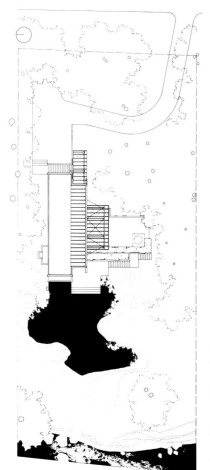

A 232 square meter house located on the slopes of a mountain valley in West Vancouver. Occupied by the architects, initially as residence and studio, the house was intended to be a speculative development which would initiate their practice in a new community.

Site
The steeply sloping site, 26 meters wide by 68.5 meters deep, is heavily forested with mature cedar, hemlock, fir, and big-leaf maple. Rogers Creek runs along the bottom of the slope 17 meters below the street above.

Design
The design was shaped by two major considerations: the mild but frequently overcast and rainy climate, and the steeply sloping site.
To not only occupy the site, but make it accessible, the house was organized on three levels in an elongated plan which 'bridges' from the top to the bottom of the slope. Each level is connected directly to an exterior space, part of a terraced series of south-facing garden or forest spaces, which parallel the interior spaces of the house.
The conjunction of heavy forest, frequently overcast climate, and valley location result in the need to maximize the amount of natural light which enters the house. The section responds directly to this need. One third of the roof is glazed. The dining room rises as a double-storey volume in the center of the plan to flood the main level of the house with light.

A large canopy over the south-facing terrace adjacent to this level, designed to make this area usable during periods of rain, is glazed to avoid shading the large window openings below it.
As a final gesture in the interests of natural light a large pond has been created at the bottom of the site to reflect the light of the sky above back up into the interior of the house.

Construction
In response to a strict budget the configuration of the house has been limited to a largely undeveloped rectangular box. Within this box four heavy timber columns divide the interior into major and minor bays. The surrounding envelope is conventional wood framing on a concrete foundation. Secondary elements, such as exterior canopies and interior guard and handrails are painted steel. A reinforced concrete-masonry fireplace provides seismic bracing for the open heavy timber frame.

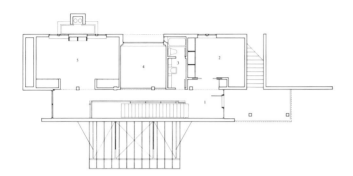

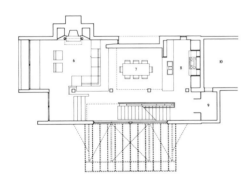

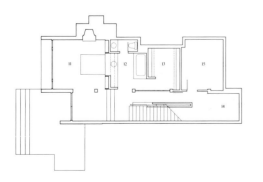

1 entry	9 pantry
2 bedroom	10 crawl space
3 bathroom	11 master bedroom
4 open to below	12 master bath
5 studio	13 closet
6 living room	14 laundry
7 dining room	15 furnace room
8 kitchen	

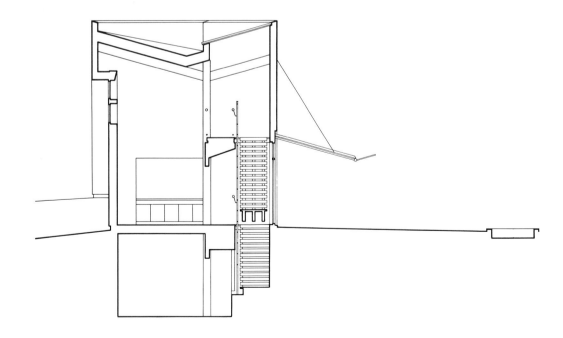

Porter / Vandenbosch Renovation
Toronto, Ontario
1985

After years as a rental property, this traditional Toronto house, circa 1910, was purchased by a contractor as his personal residence. The house was in a dilapidated state and had several *ad hoc* additions attached to it. Construction consisted of an uninsulated double wythe brick exterior shell with a wood-framed interior structure.

Design
In an attempt to return the structure to its original simplicity and clarity, the exterior additions were removed. The interior was gutted, leaving only the brick shell.
The inner surface of the shell was reconstructed to achieve contemporary building envelope standards. Window and door openings were refurbished using traditional details, albeit in an edited rather than literal manner.
An entirely new interior, framed in steel, was then inserted into the shell, juxtaposing the material and spatial qualities of old and new.

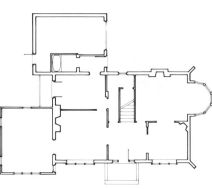

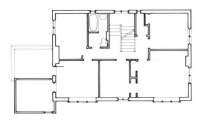

before

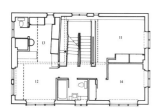

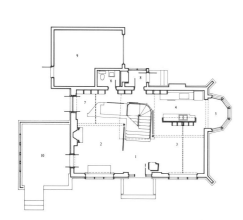

after

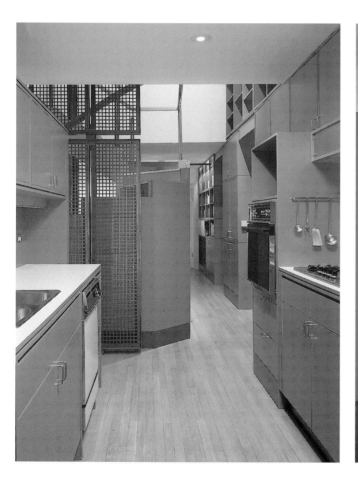

Appleton House
Victoria, British Columbia
1985

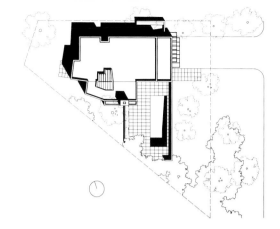

A simple but generous house, substantial in feeling, with outdoor swimming pool for a couple with three young children. Size and construction conform to a contemporary context of conventional speculatively built "subdivision" houses.

Site
A flat, irregularly shaped lot located in Rockland, an old neighborhood in central Victoria containing a great variety of houses ranging from turn-of-the-century mansions to postwar bungalows.

Design
To achieve a feeling of "substance" within conventional means, it was decided that planning and construction must be straight- forward and that the character of the house would have to be defined through large simple gestures.
To this end, a single large volume in which all of the activities of the family as a whole would take place was located toward the south. Rooms for individual use: parents' bedroom and den on the main level, and children's bedrooms and playroom on the upper level, were then aligned along the northern edge of this volume.
The large volume, almost a hall or great room in traditional terms, was then subtly subdivided by a single monumental column into living and dining areas — the singleness and overwhelming physical presence of the column complementing the scale of the volume.

Four irregular brackets, which form an over-sized capital for the column, break through the roof of the house to create a fragmented skylight. Against this dynamic gesture, an archaically proportioned Rumford fireplace centers the living area and acts to ground the movement of the space.

Construction
Within the limits of the project, conventional wood frame construction is the only feasible building technology available in Victoria. Exterior walls are finished in a heavily textured stucco and interior walls and ceilings are painted gypsum board. Floors are oak, in living, dining, and kitchen areas, with carpet in the remainder of the house.
Through the manipulation of scale and detail these materials are used to create an overall feeling of substance. Special elements such as the column, fireplace, and pivot doors, as well as the great room are oversized while everything else is reduced to the most conventional proportion. Special construction details are also used to give physical credibility to what in other contexts are the humblest of building materials: a combination parapet flashing/ plaster stop allows the stucco finish to end at the very top of the wall so that exterior stucco masses are defined abstractly against the sky: the house appearing carved from a solid monolith. Interior volumes are defined without recourse to conventional "edgings" so that the monolithic

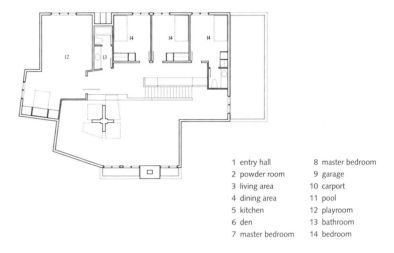

character implied on the exterior is maintained. The energy systems of the house are a mixture of the "state-of-the-art" and the archaic rediscovered. As gas is not available in Victoria, the house is heated electrically by radiant panels of thin metallic foil located in ceilings. Fresh air is supplied via an air-to-air heat exchanger to all rooms. In the great room , which receives a full 50% of the fresh air of the house, the air is passed within the column to mix with the warm air which collects below the skylight, counteracting any stratification which might occur due to the height of the room. The fireplace design is based on the firebox developed by Sir Benjamin Thompson, Count Rumford, in the eighteenth century. This design, in conjunction with some modern refinements, maximizes the distribution of heat from an open fire by direct and re-emitted radiation, rather than by (fan driven) air circulation from a fully enclosed fire, as is the case with most "energy efficient" fireplaces today.

1 entry hall	8 master bedroom
2 powder room	9 garage
3 living area	10 carport
4 dining area	11 pool
5 kitchen	12 playroom
6 den	13 bathroom
7 master bedroom	14 bedroom

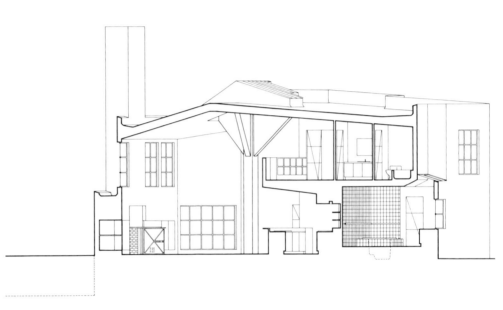

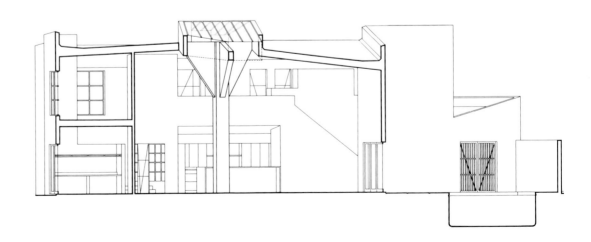

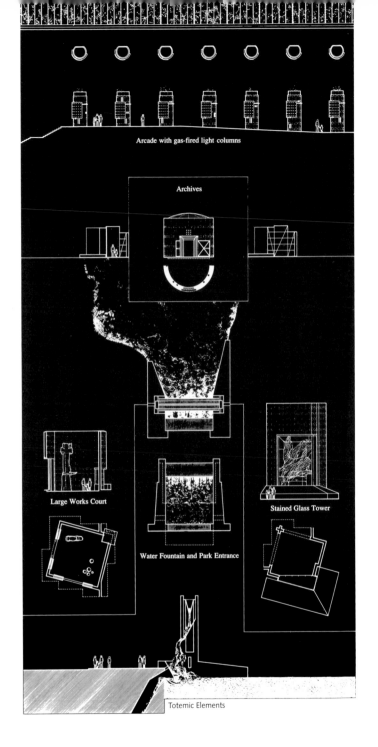

Arcade with gas-fired light columns

Archives

Large Works Court

Stained Glass Tower

Water Fountain and Park Entrance

Totemic Elements

Canadian Clay & Glass Gallery
Competition
Waterloo, Ontario
1986

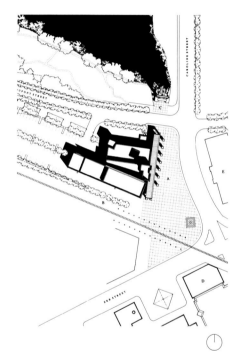

Museum Function

The Gallery has three essential functions related to the art object or cultural artifact. These are the physical preservation and storage of the objects; their display and interpretation within a cultural or intellectual context; and their presentation in a manner facilitating emotional contact or contemplation. Beyond these aspects is an important requirement for the expression in the civic context of the Gallery's role as a cultural, intellectual, and entertainment facility.

In the design of the building these functions are emphasized and symbolized by certain totemic elements which place the spectator and artifact in a specific, intensified architectural relationship.

Metaphor of Transformation

The design of the Gallery is informed by the idea of the origin of ceramics and glass in an 'alchemical' or transformational process from earth, through fire, to finished object. Similarly, the making of art is linked to the seeing and experiencing of art through an "act of mind", a transformation by imagination which connects spectator with artist.

This transformation is expressed in the Gallery by the central space which connects the physical process of the glassblowing studio and the intellectual ordering and interpretation of the display/storage wall with the contemplative experience of the galleries.

Urban Design Intentions

The site is situated at the periphery of Waterloo's downtown area, as is the future site of the Waterloo City Hall. These two places mark two significant edges of the city core. The design of the Gallery and its public square is intended to describe this edge condition and form a civic space of equal importance to the future City Hall.

A major axial connection is made between the Gallery, Seagram's Museum, and the proposed park gate, reiterating the idea of a cultural and recreational precinct relating the two museums with the park and lake The museum square thus formed makes a terminus to the pedestrian path from the University of Waterloo and a gateway to the city center.

1 gas-fired light columns
2 arcade
3 lobby
4 information / ticket desk
5 cloakroom
6 telephones
7 gift shop
8 tea room
9 tea room terrace
10 orientation lecture theatre
11 viewing corridor
12 large works gallery
13 stained glass gallery
14 glazed feature wall
15 shipping & receiving
16 storage
17 workshop
18 adjucation
19 hydraulic platform lift
20 glassblowing studio

21 mechanical & electrical room
22 roof
23 library
24 reception
25 staff washrooms
26 boardroom
27 copy room
28 director
29 secretary
30 curator
31 educator
32 docents
33 open to below
34 storage

Totemic Elements

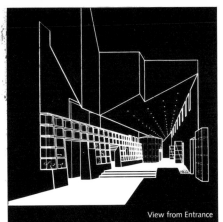

View from Entrance

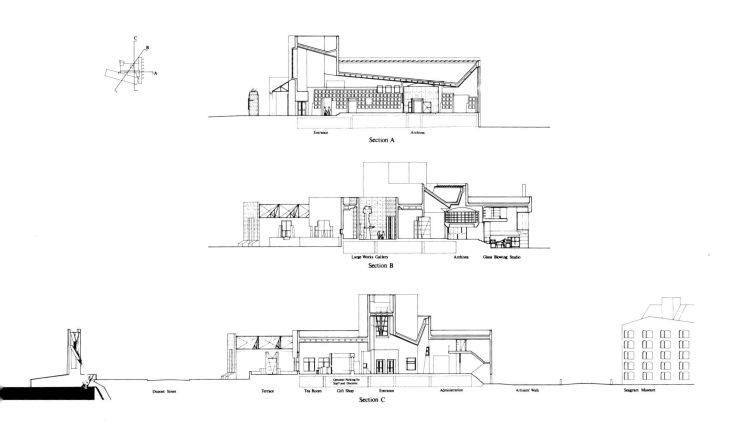

Section A

Entrance   Archives

Large Works Gallery   Archives   Glass Blowing Studio

Section B

Dupont Street   Terrace   Tea Room   Gift Shop   Entrance   Administration   Artisans' Walk   Seagram Museum

Optional Parking for
Staff and Docents

Section C

Kustin House

Los Angeles, California
1986

A 325 square meter house including a large workshop for the owner, a maker of cane fly-fishing rods. Construction, scheduled for the fall of 1988, was to be phased over a number of years as it was the owner's intention to fabricate many of the components of the house himself.

Site

An open grassy lot, 24 meters wide by 53 meters deep, located on a ridge in the Woodland Hills area of Los Angeles. From the street the site slopes very steeply down to provide panoramic views of the valley below and further ranges of low hills to the west.

Design

Three principal considerations shaped our design: The first had to do with the climate of the region which is characterized by long summers of extreme heat and intense light. The historical response to these conditions has been an architecture of large wall surfaces with limited numbers of small openings, of high walled courts, and of broad shading devices. The second had to do with the simple but powerful condition of the steeply sloping site; a condition only fully revealed when registered against the constructional absolutes of horizontal and vertical. The third had to do with the ancient, yet highly refined, craft of the owner; and the recognition of the ability of singular artifacts to effect the environment in which they are located.

The house, itself, is essentially earth related; a stucco cube intersected by the slope of the site. Exterior spaces are limited to a few paved roof terraces to the south and west and a shaded garden court, enclosed by high walls, to the north. Window openings are either small, deeply recessed, or shaded. Interiors are simple planar volumes.

The primary exception to this predominantly elemental character is a wood and glass interstice which bisects the house in the direction of the slope. Here stairs fall within an increasing rift between the halves of the house to "reveal" the site and make its presence central to the experience of the house. Here, too, an assortment of wood constructions animates the interior. A vaguely anthropomorphic column, hollow, constructed of radial splines like the cane rods made by the owner provides a duct for the destratification of air within the three story volume of the rift. A pair of gently arched bridges span the rift, tying the two halves of the house together.

Other constructions enliven the perimeter of the house: the north garden court is inhabited by a smaller column whose upraised arms support a glazed eating porch. To the west, bracketed outriggers stretch to shade terraces and the large openings of living and dining room. These outriggers, half sail and half fishing rod in conception, provide a dynamic contrast to the mute static masses of the house, and at the same time signal the unusual craft of the owner.

Construction

For the most part construction of the house is
comprised of conventional wood framing on
a concrete grade beam and pile foundation.
Exterior walls are stucco, roof terraces and
patios are concrete, interior walls are painted
gypsum board. Within this general envelope
special elements such as the column, bridges,
and roof framing of the rift, the eating porch in
the north garden court, doors, window frames,
and most cabinetry items were to be fabricated
by the owner from a variety of woods.
The large sunshade elements above the living
and dining room terraces to the west are a
composite wood and steel construction rigged
with a specially woven sunshade fabric.

1 entry hall
2 powder room
3 back entry / laundry
4 garage
5 living room
6 terrace
7 bridge
8 dining room
9 kitchen
10 eating nook
11 garden court

12 pool
13 den
14 open to below
15 master bedroom
16 closet
17 master bath
18 sitting room
19 washroom
20 guest bedroom
21 workshop
22 utility room

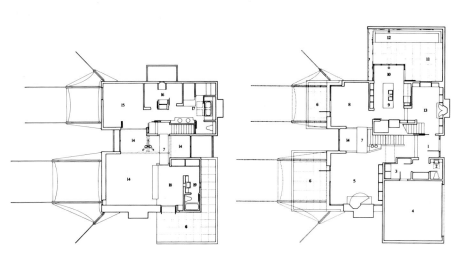

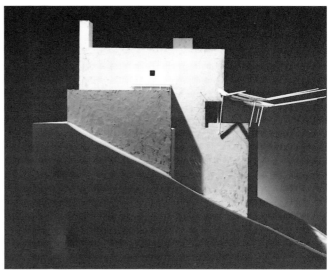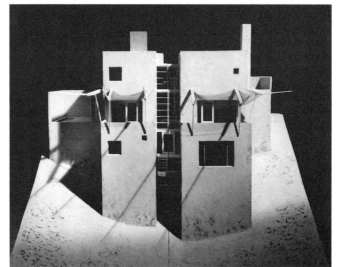

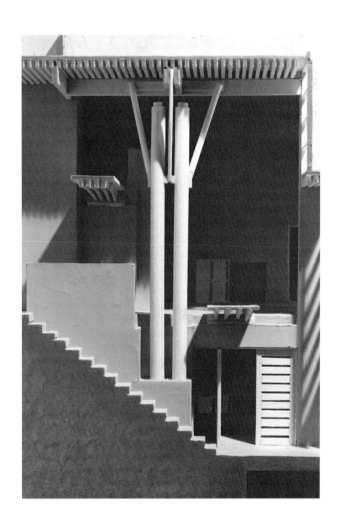

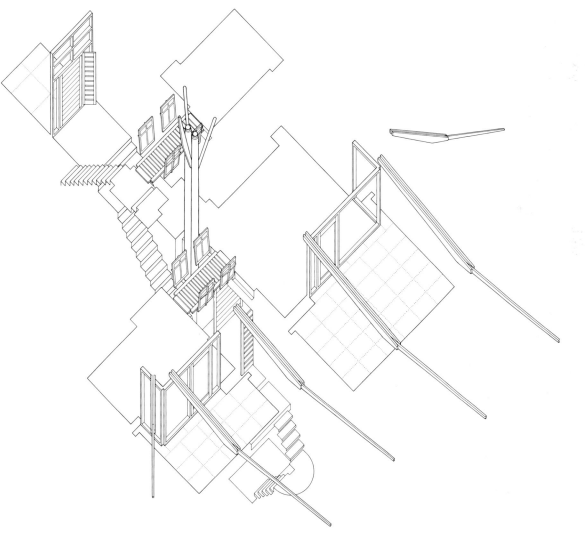

55

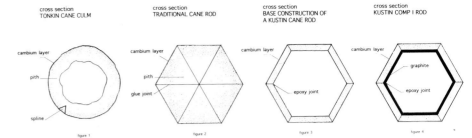

cross section
TONKIN CANE CULM

cross section
TRADITIONAL CANE ROD

cross section
BASE CONSTRUCTION OF
A KUSTIN CANE ROD

cross section
KUSTIN COMP I ROD

An inside look at the construction of the Kustin comp cane rods

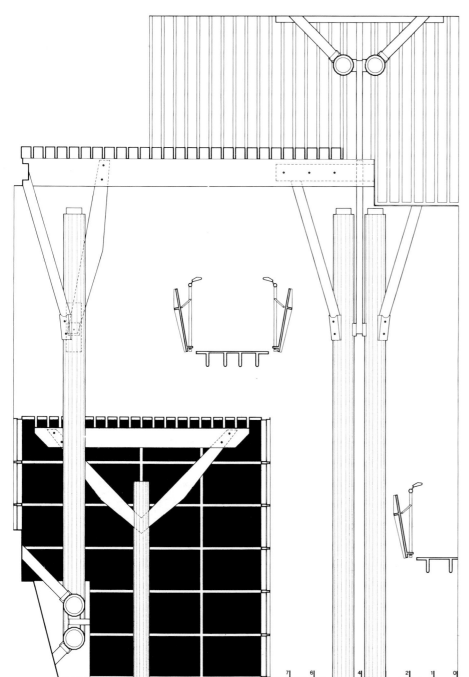

57

Seabird Island School

Agassiz, British Columbia
1988

1 community buildings
2 village common space
3 bridge
4 dry creek bed
5 fire pit
6 Seabird Island School
7 outdoor play area
8 traditional pit house
9 teaching gardens
10 salmon drying racks
11 bus & passenger drop-off
12 parking

The Seabird Island Band believes that the first purpose of their educational program is to promote and enhance the culture, language and way of life of the Salish people of the Pacific Northwest. Thus, a fairly conventional school program, providing an area of 2190 square meters which includes 10 elementary and secondary classrooms (with provision for four additional secondary classrooms), a kindergarten, administrative areas, and a gymnasium/community hall, was significantly informed by community values. A clear interface between the school and village was essential, not only in making the school a vital part of the community, but also in encouraging the active participation of the community in the school's daily operation.

Site

Seabird Island is a large island located in the Fraser River, approximately 120 kilometers east of Vancouver. Mountains of the Coastal Range of British Columbia tower over the river valley on all sides. The interior of the island consists of a large open field used for agriculture. Individual houses ring the lightly wooded perimeter.

Located at the downstream end of the island the community buildings are loosely organized around a grassed square in an incipient 'U'-shaped configuration, open to the north.

Design

To strengthen and further define the emerging structure and character of the community center, the school was sited along the open northern edge of the existing grassed square. By making the school an integral part of the village common space, interaction between the school and the community is clearly encouraged. At the same time, the extreme winter winds which are funneled between the mountains down the river valley from the north are now mediated by the large mass of the building allowing a more favourable microclimate to develop on the southern, community side of the school. Within this protected zone, outdoor play areas, teaching gardens, and other community facilities extend from the school edge to integrate with the village green space.

The continuity of the public realm with the school, established by the siting of the building, is further reinforced through its organization. Classrooms, as well as the main entrance, are laced along the southern face, each opening to a collective porch and the play areas beyond creating a permeable and active edge along the village green. Within, and directly accessible from this southern edge via the main entrance, a central common area acts as the physical core of the building. Immediately beyond, on the northerly path from the village and green into the school, the gymnasium/community hall provides a final destination in the newly created sequence of public spaces. To each side the elementary and secondary wings of the school are organized along open library/resource areas. Consistent with the educational philosophy of the Band, few distinctions have been

made between areas specifically designed for staff and those for students, allowing a significant overlap to occur in the commons and the resource areas. Covered outdoor play areas for general use are provided to the south along the porch, and specifically for the kindergarten, to the east under a large canopy.

In mediating between the extreme winter winds from the north and the favourable exposure toward the village green on the south, the mass and scale of the school undergo a transformation. On the north, large sculptural volumes, vaguely zoomorphic in character, are closed diverting the winds much like the mountains which surround the site. To the south the scale is small, the building open under generous eaves. A complex, more tectonic quality not present in the sculptural forms of the north is introduced through the use of a variety of struts, beams and trellises which animate this edge suggesting the potential richness of community life.

Construction

Heavy timber post and beam construction is the traditional building technique of the Natives of the Pacific Northwest. The structure of the Seabird Island School, a modern 'engineered' form of this technique, is comprised of paralam columns and beams with steel connections on a reinforced concrete grade-beam and pile foundation. As much of this structure was erected by members of the band who are not experienced in large scale construction

methods, a detailed framing model was made to supplement conventional construction documents. Walls and roofs are clad, generally, in cedar shingles, the traditional cladding material of the region. As they weather, these shingles will shade naturally from a soft silver-grey to a deep red-brown depending upon orientation and exposure. In this way the sculptural volumes of the north will be enriched and subtly exaggerated. Under the broad eaves of the south and east, walls are clad in translucent white stained plywood panels to increase luminosity and proved a contrast to the weathered character of the north much as the pearly interior of an oyster shell contrasts with the rugged grey tones of its exterior.

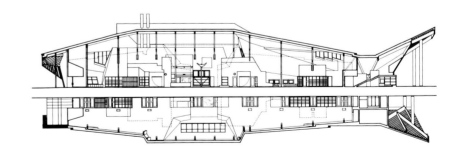

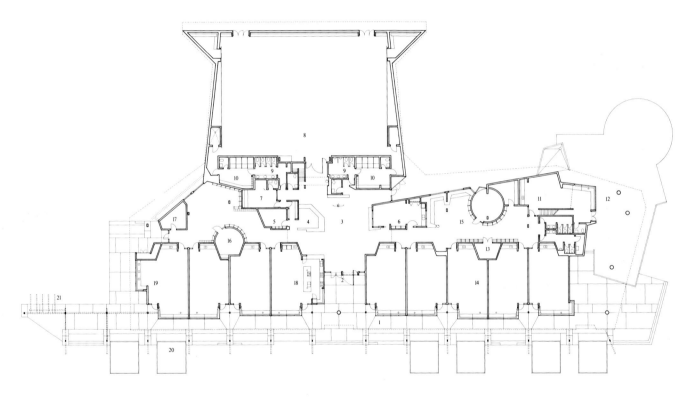

1 covered porch	8 gym /community hall	15 library / resource area
2 entrance	9 washrooms	16 reading room
3 common area	10 showers / change rooms	17 workroom
4 reception	11 kindergarten	18 home economics room
5 principal	12 covered play area	19 science room
6 staff room	13 storage	20 teaching gardens
7 health / counselling	14 classroom	21 drying racks

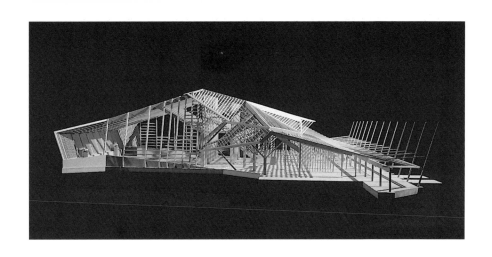

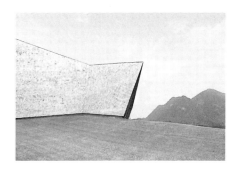

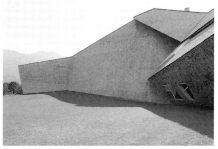

Cross section through entrance and gym
Cross section through elementary wing
East elevation

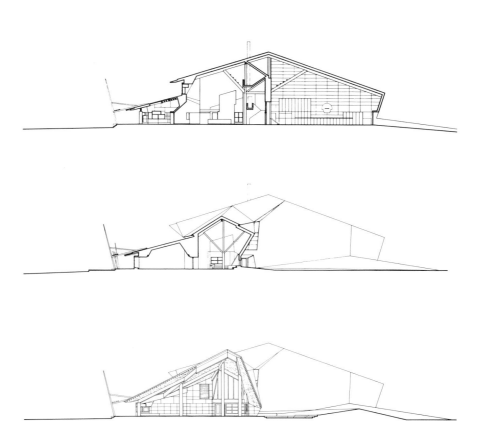

Canadian Clay & Glass Gallery
Waterloo, Ontario
1988

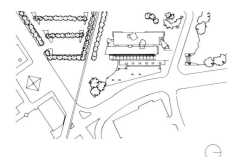

In October and November of 1986 a limited national competition was held for the design of a new gallery for the display of contemporary Canadian clay and glass art. This gallery was to be located on a site adjacent to the Seagram Museum, donated by the City of Waterloo, Ontario. Funding was to be provided equally by the Government of Canada, the Government of Ontario, and private donations. Due to delays in the release of certain components of this funding, development of the competition design was postponed until the beginning of 1989. By this time construction costs had increased to such a degree that it was necessary to substantially reduce the scope of the original building program.

Revisions to the Program
To reduce the scope of the original program to bring the 1990 costs of the project into line with the original 1986 budget approximately one-third of the original building area of 2500 square meters had to be eliminated. To this end the glassblowing studio and lecture theater were deleted and components within the support areas were reduced substantially. Architecturally the deletion of the glassblowing studio made the direct expression of the process from making, through collection and selection, to the display of art no longer appropriate. The irregular central space of the original design within which this process was made evident was therefore eliminated to further reduce and simplify the final design.

The revelation of this process of 'certification' of the art object provided a basis for the critical understanding of institutionalized culture. In the revised final design the actual manner in which the gallery spaces were developed would have to provide this type of critical context. Provisions for substantial future expansion were also deleted from the program although limited additional support facilities are projected for an area to the west of the present building.

The Nature of Gallery Space
The modern stereotype of the art gallery space is the white cube; a pure white space, lit artificially, with no connection to the world beyond. This stereotype has arisen naturally as a response to curatorial interests as well as to the drive toward abstraction characteristic of avant garde painting and sculpture of the post-war period. The fundamental difficulty with this view is the tendency of this type of space to place 'art-on-a-pedestal' — in a sense to turn works of art into pseudo-sacred objects divorced from everyday life.

The design of the Canadian Clay and Glass Gallery challenges the extreme isolation of this stereotype. First, the gallery interiors are strongly connected to the outside world: Natural light from skylights and windows articulates the order of the gallery spaces. An exterior courtyard brings daily and seasonal cycles into the gallery interior. Stained glass is displayed against the background of exterior

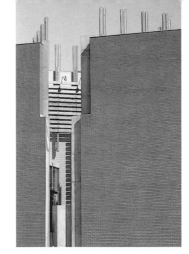

views so that it may be animated by changing light and movement. Second, the construction of the gallery interiors is not abstract: building materials are directly expressed; details reveal the layers of construction — the building up of roof and wall assemblies — and articulate the relationships of materials to each other. In this way the art objects which are displayed (as well as the architecture within which they are displayed) are connected to normal experiences, so that they may be understood to be part of everyday life.

Construction

The construction of the gallery reveals a simple hierarchy of building materials: Totemic elements — the courtyard, small works and tower galleries as well as the gas fired light columns — are reinforced concrete. The roof and second floor of the surrounding construction consist of a heavy timber deck supported by steel beam and purlin framing. Concrete masonry bearing walls, exposed to the interior support the roof and floor assemblies. On the exterior, these walls are clad with brick veneer, detailed at door and window openings to express the composite nature of the wall. Door and window frames are stained wood. The main floor is a reinforced concrete platform, left exposed, supported by a reinforced concrete grade beam and pile foundation.

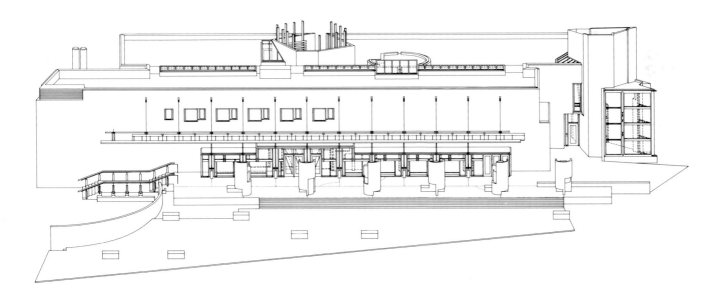

1   gas fired light columns
2   entry vestibule
3   lobby
4   information and ticket desk
5   cloakroom
6   gift shop
7   tea room
8   main gallery
9   tower gallery
10 small works gallery
11 courtyard gallery
12 demonstration and adjudication
13 support facilities
14 mechanical and electrical room

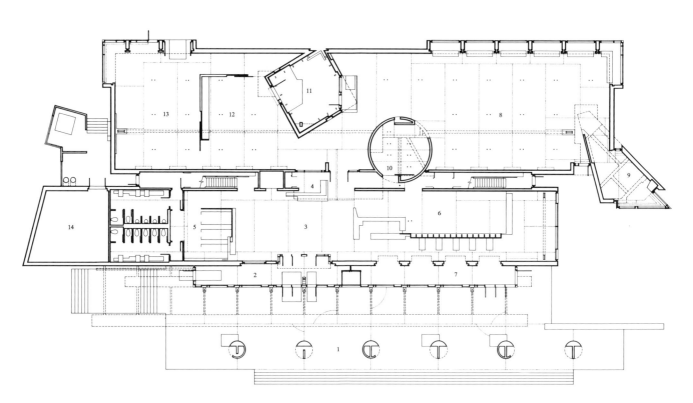

1 secretary and reception
2 director
3 curator
4 educator
5 docents
6 janitor
7 library and archives
8 reading rood and board room
9 librarian
10 workroom
11 kitchenette
12 open to below
13 mechanical room

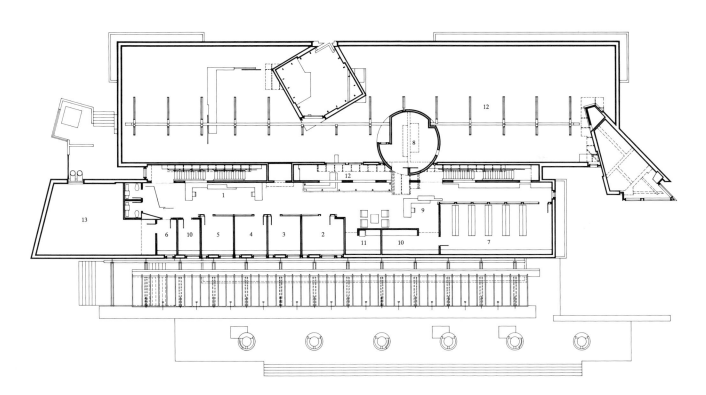

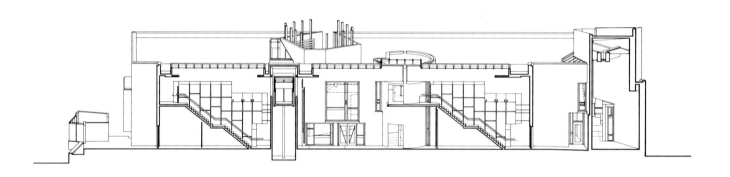

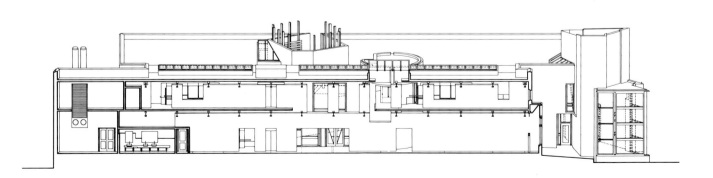

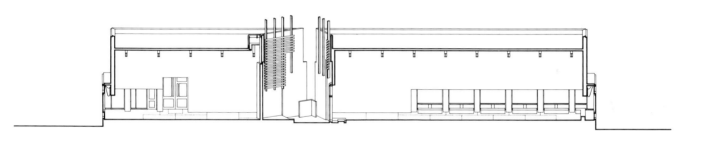

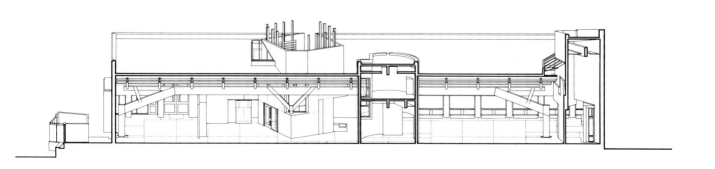

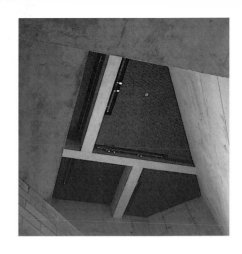

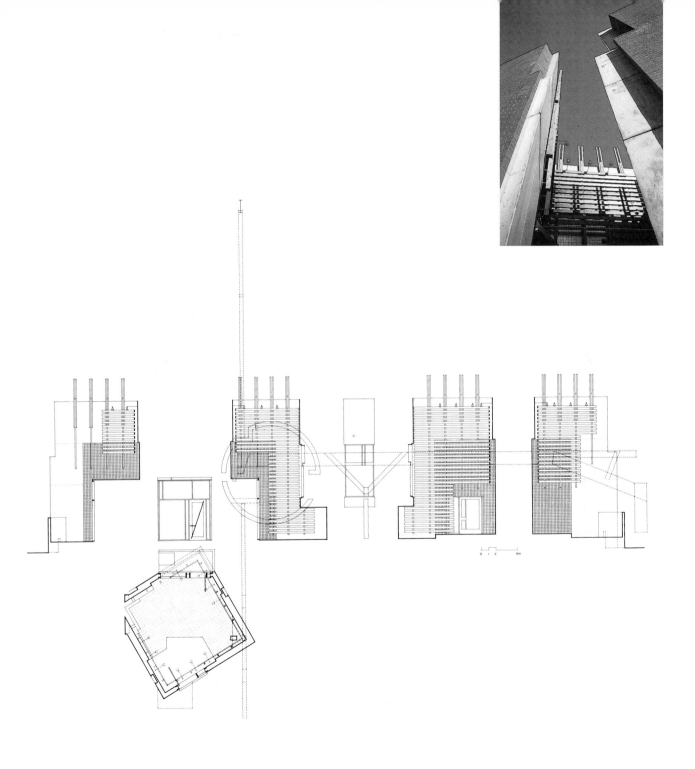

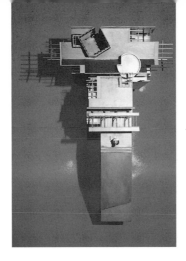

Post-Design Model Study

Subsequent to the completion of the design of the project a model study was undertaken to continue to explore certain of the formal principles of the design.

The model is comprised of an irregular section taken through the center of the building. The partial nature of the model allows characteristics of the design, such as the play of complex linear constructions against simple geometric volumes and the layering of components within building assemblies, to be made more explicit. Further, and largely independent of the original design, the partial nature of the model suggests unexpected formal possibilities having to do with the densely centered but open-ended composition, or the juxtaposition of complete and fragmentary forms. In this way the ideas and lessons of the original design are extrapolated so that they may begin to inform future work.

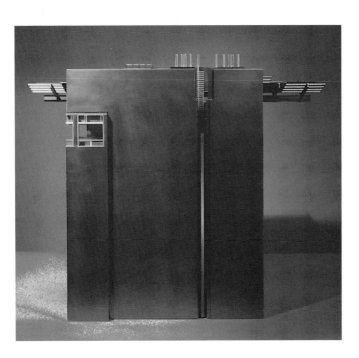

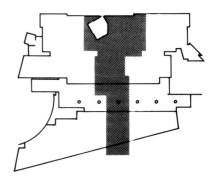

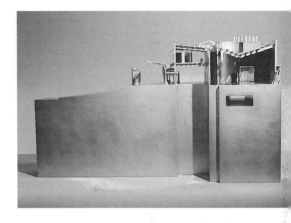

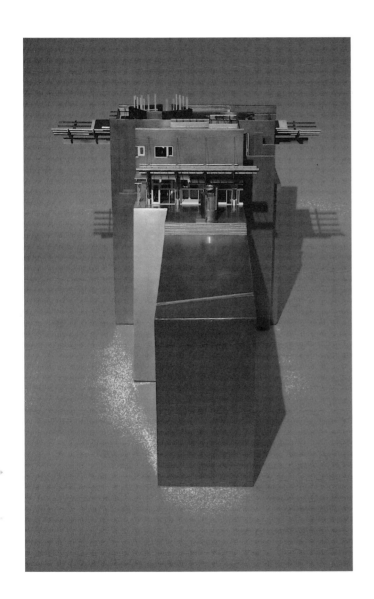

Newton Library
Surrey, British Columbia
1990

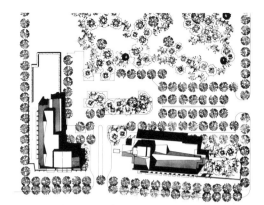

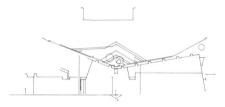

A 1,486 square meter branch library serving one of five town centres in the municipality of Surrey, a low density suburb of Vancouver, British Columbia.

Site

Six acres, shared with a recreation facility for the elderly adjacent to a neighbourhood retail centre and surrounded by existing, and projected, low density residential neighbourhoods. Prior to development the site was largely covered by a scrub deciduous forest of red alder mixed with small patches of the original evergreen rain forest of cedar, hemlock, and fir which is characteristic of the region.

Design

The library, recreation facility and associated parking areas were located on the site so as to retain as much of the original evergreen patches as possible. New deciduous trees were planted in a regular grid within parking areas to create a clear juxtaposition between the apparently random nature of the original forest patches and the simple geometric order of buildings and parking areas.

The library was located along the south edge of the site. In order to give it the presence appropriate to a public institution adrift in the suburban sea of 'strip malls' and residential subdivisions, as well as to give some definition to the street, the height of the single storey perimeter walls to the north and south was exaggerated. Not only does this give the

building greater presence on the street, it also allows large amounts of natural light to enter the building in controlled ways. The south side is layered and shaped to modify the sometimes harsh south sun while the north glass 'curtain wall' allows the soft north light to fill the interior with a quiet luminosity. The resultant sidedness of the building is one of its primary architectural characteristics. The transparency of the building also helps to communicate its purpose to the surrounding community. While the perimeter walls to the north and south are exaggerated in height to give the library a public presence, the scale of the entrance to the west, adjacent to the principal vehicular access to the site, is compressed, even intimate. This compression or valley in the cross-section runs the entire length of the building maintaining the scale established at the entrance along the principal circulation spine of the plan. The inward sloping ceiling planes which result help drive the light which enters through the high side walls deep into the interior.

This valley also works in conjunction with a complementary pitched attic space above the roof to provide a plenum which houses the major air distribution ducts leading from a mechanical penthouse located directly above the entrance. The cross-section of this attic space diminishes in conjunction with a reduction in the number and size of ducts as it moves away from the penthouse. The changing intersection of attic and valley results in a cross-slope which drains the entire roof to each end of the building. Here water is directed through large galvanized steel scuppers into rock filled catchment areas on grade and then allowed to permeate back into the site.

Construction
Sticks and stones / droops, lumps and horns
The construction of the building begins with the natural sticks and stones of the region — a heavy timber (glu-lam) structural frame on a concrete foundation. The tectonic qualities of this construction establish the primary character of the building shell.

However, because the light of the Vancouver area can be very soft, even weak, under the frequently overcast skies of winter, the robust light absorbing character of heavy timber and concrete, in themselves, are not appropriate to distribute natural light into a relatively deep floor plate. For this reason a complementary clad construction of painted gypsum board on the interior, and stucco on the exterior was overlaid on portions of the tectonic frame of the building. The cladding of ceiling and walls acts to reflect light from the edges to the centre of the building. As well, this droopy ceiling acts in conjunction with the lumpy attic of the roof to house and distribute the mechanical and electrical systems of the building.

Where its luminous and enclosing characteristics are not required the layer of cladding is feathered out to its own thickness, eventually giving way to exposed construction. This allows the tectonic, more durable parts of the building to extend outside as a rain canopy. The relationship of these two types of construction is further developed by a number of horns, both inside and out. These assertive shapes allow the clad construction to take on a more figural quality which enables it to act as a more positive counterpoint to the robust quality of timber and concrete. In this way a dialectic of construction types energizes the architectural expression of the building.

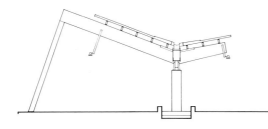

1 circulation desk
2 multipurpose room
3 circulation workroom
4 shipping / receiving
5 janitor's room
6 circulation supervisor
7 staff room
8 adults' library workroom
9 adults' librarian
10 chief librarian
11 computer room
12 children's librarian
13 children's library workroom
14 seminar room

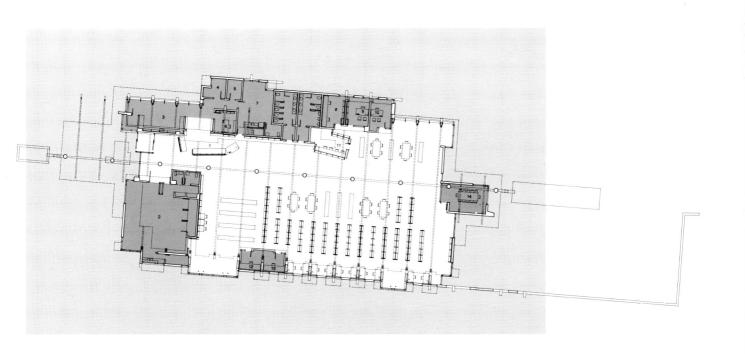

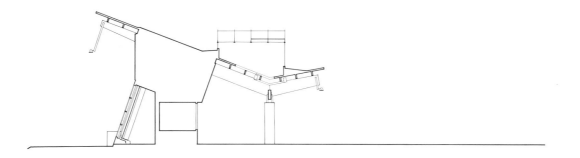

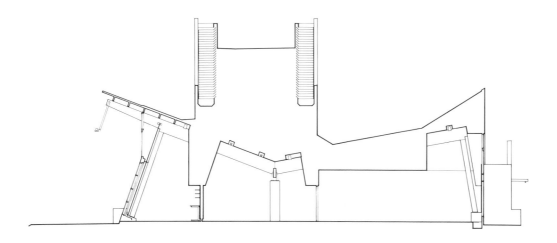

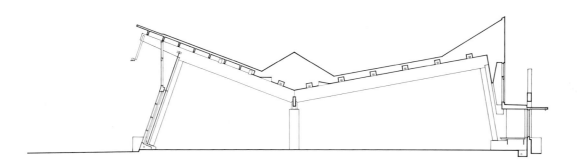

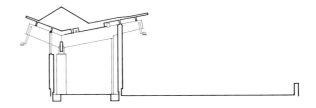

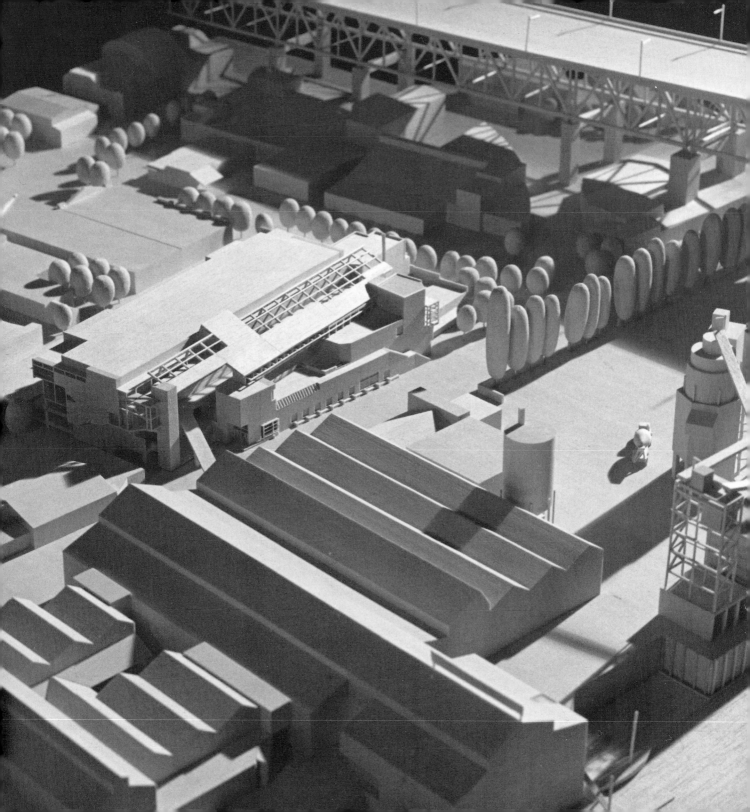

Emily Carr College of Art and Design

Vancouver, British Columbia

1991

An additional 5,575 square meters of studios and associated spaces for Emily Carr College, and 255 parking stalls for general use, to be located across the street from the existing college facility. The studio spaces, which constitute the largest component of the new building, are for the use of students in painting, sculpture, ceramics, multimedia art, graphic design, industrial design, and electronic communications design. Associated with these spaces are a variety of support areas, including academic offices, workshops, and seminar rooms. A library and a 175 seat lecture theater, intended for use by both the college and the general public, are also included in the program.

Site

Located on Granville Island, in central Vancouver, the site is delimited by Johnston Street to the north, a small park to the east, and a group of existing heavy timber buildings housing galleries and workshops to the south and west. Across Johnston street is the existing Emily Carr College of Art and Design and a concrete plant.

Design

Because subsurface conditions on Granville Island make building the parking garage entirely below grade impracticable, the fundamental urban design problem is to position a college building on top of a two-storey parking garage while maintaining the small scale,

pedestrian-oriented character of Granville Island. A related concern is the importance of establishing a direct and comfortable relationship between the college and the street in spite of the elevational difference thus created. The internal organization of the school is governed by the need to maximize flexibility of use and organization of the major studio spaces, and to develop the non-programmed spaces as areas of social activity, hopefully promoting random, daily exchange amongst students and faculty. The general distribution of the building's spaces is driven largely by an attempt to minimize the building's apparent bulk and the impact of the parking garage on the character of surrounding streets. The garage is hidden from view by construction on three sides; along Old Bridge Street and Railspur Alley existing buildings have been preserved to screen it, and along Johnston Street the college library obscures the garage while providing a publicly accessible amenity at street level. The library is developed as though an autonomous institution, provided with its own street entrance, with the object of fostering pedestrian activity on the street and drawing attention to the public nature of this part of the college. Above, the majority of the college program area, and the building's bulk, is contained in a two-storey bar set well back from the streets, the upper level occupied by the traditional fine art disciplines, and the lower by the professionally oriented design

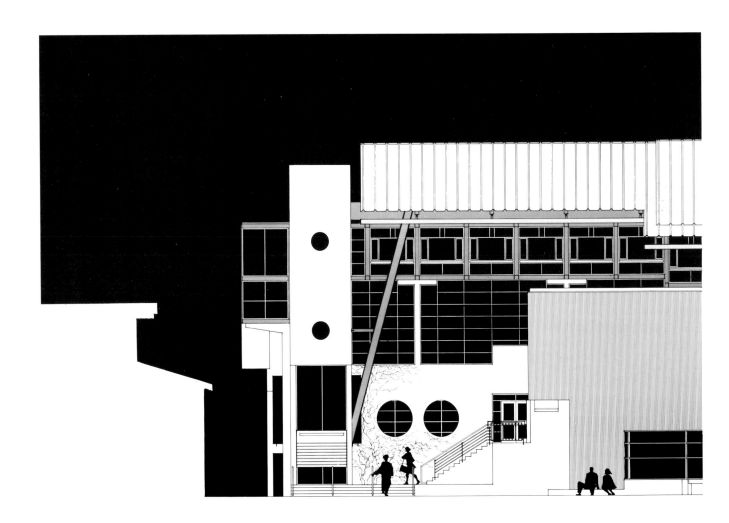

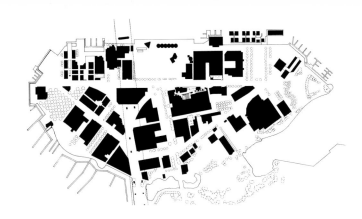

disciplines. The remaining program components are smaller scale elements, academic offices and seminar rooms, which are distributed in a somewhat freer manner above the library, around a double height, glazed concourse space. The effect of this organization is the creation of a more permeable edge between the major spaces of the college and Johnston Street. To further diminish the apparent mass of the building, service elements, such as exit stairs, elevators, and mechanical rooms, have been held proud of the main building volume, introducing detail and complexity at the building's edges.

The organization of the school about the central, street-like concourse provides the facility with a common space that may be used for exhibitions and other public events, as well as for general building circulation. Both roof and wall glazing in this area is operable, rendering it, in favourable weather, an outdoor space contiguous with Johnston Street.

The use of colour is both a response to the prevailing decorative protocol of the island, and an attempt to minimize the apparent size of the building. The major volumes are clad in galvanized sheet metal; being unassertive and "neutral" in colour, it is intended that these surfaces will reflect ambient light in a diffuse manner, and recede visually. At grade, however, bright colours are applied to the small scale steel trim components of the cladding system, resulting in a linear application of decorative colour similar in effect to the

painting of facias and pipe rails typical of Granville Island. In this manner, the parts of the building most immediate to the pedestrian become the most detailed and visually dominant.

Construction

The building construction is primarily reinforced concrete, with the roof and its supporting structure framed in steel. As is typical on Granville Island, corrugated metal is generally used for the cladding of insulated walls. Because of the utilitarian nature of studio space, and because of the 'industrial' character of the prevailing mode of construction on the island, construction and services are typically left exposed, and the detailing of cladding attempts to be direct and frank.

Barnes House
Nanaimo, British Columbia
1992

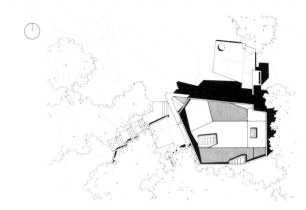

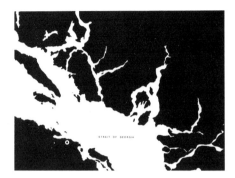

Site
The edge of an open rocky outcrop within a generally forested five acre parcel of land which overlooks the Strait of Georgia and the mainland of British Columbia to the north and along the rocky shoreline of Vancouver Island to the northwest.

Design
The Barnes house represents the most current expression of our architectural investigation, which has been ongoing for the past decade. It is founded on the following objectives:

A search for the particular: In the context of the increasing dominance of the general within our culture, differentiation and the creation of the particular become increasingly meaningful. Our search for the particular begins with the givens, the base data, of a project — a search for what we call the 'found potential' of a project. In the case of the Barnes house the 'found potential' is most evidently the site. Here the site is understood to be not only the rocky outcrop upon which the house is situated and the surrounding vegetation which encompasses it but the entire region centered on the Strait of Georgia. Not only is this region clearly comprehensible as a large scaled place it is actually visible from the site.

In this context the house has been designed as a landscape focusing device — a mechanism through which the experience of this place, from the small scaled textural characteristics of the rock to the large scaled expanse of the sea, is made manifest.

A search for the 'real': Unlike historical architectural paradigms, such as classicism or modernism, which are based on 'ideals' or 'ideal types' (humanism in the first case, abstraction in the second), this search attempts a form of pragmatism — the treatment of subject matter at 'face value', without idealization. One important consequence of this attitude is that architecture is not viewed as something distinct from the natural world. As surely as the forces of nature act upon architecture, man (especially when amplified by technology) works upon nature. In this context while architecture is clearly something man-made it must also be understood to be continuous with the natural world.

The Barnes house reflects this attitude. In experiential terms it shares an irregularity and variability of space and massing that is characteristic of its site. It does so as a straightforward response to the exigencies of making a small place for man in the larger context of the natural world.

A search for heterogeneity: Both the differentiation implicit in a search for the particular and the pragmatism upon which a search for the 'real' is based lead inevitably to a condition of heterogeneity; the simultaneous presence of regular and irregular, strong and weak, etc. The Barnes house manifests this condition in formal/spatial terms. Witness the conjunction in plan and section of orthogonal and non-orthogonal geometries. Witness the figural strength of north and west elevations versus the figural weakness of south and east elevations. It also manifests this condition in material terms. Concrete, steel, wood, and stucco are each used in different ways, each in the manner in which it is most capable.

Construction

For the most part the shell of the house is comprised of conventional wood framing, stucco clad, on a reinforced concrete grade beam foundation. Three concrete columns rise within this volume to support a heavy timber roof structure. Floors are generally exposed concrete, either as a slab-on-grade in the lower level or as a topping on wood framing in the main level. Steel is used as a counterpoint to the monolithic concrete and stucco clad wood framing, as elaborated connections between concrete and heavy timber, as railings at stairs, and as a canopy over the entrance and large window facing northwest. This canopy, which is made of 10 millimeters thick steel plate, cantilevers 3.7 meters over the openings it shelters. Interior wall surfaces are painted gypsum board.

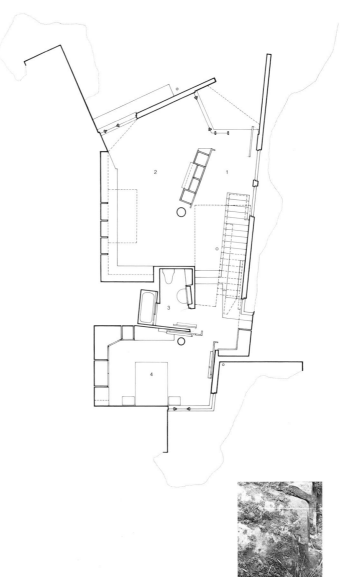

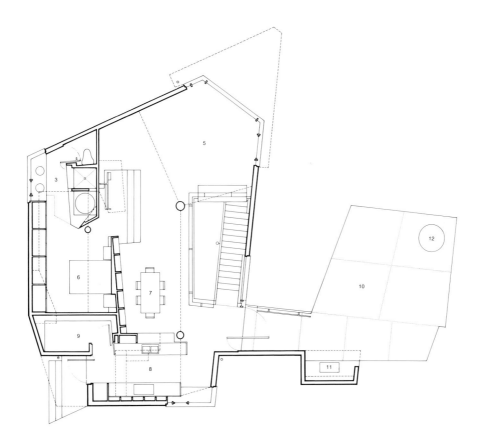

1 entry
2 studio
3 bathroom
4 guest room
5 living room
6 master bedroom
7 dining room
8 kitchen
9 utility
10 terrace
11 barbecue
12 fire pit

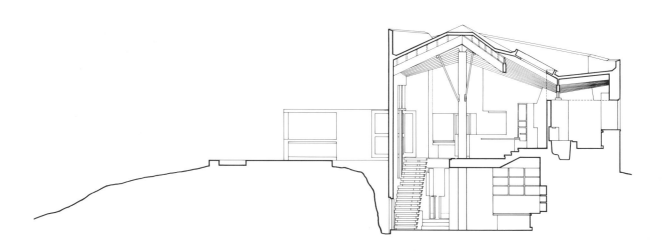

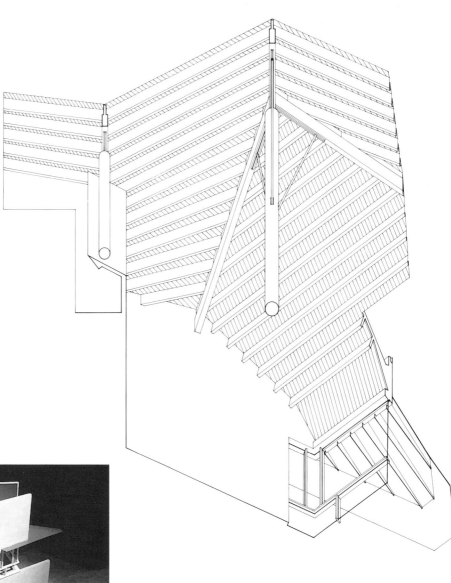

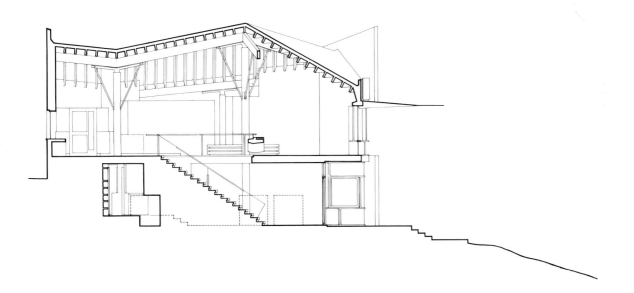

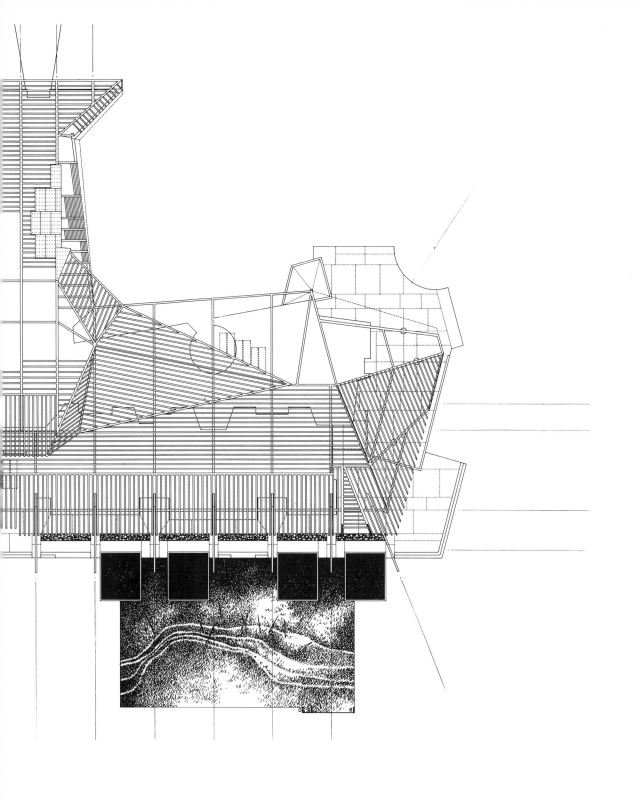

Postscript
Kenneth Frampton

John and Patricia Patkau are two young Canadian architects whose achievements are all the more refreshing because of their discretely tectonic character. The quality of this work suggests once again that we would do well to turn our attention to the periphery, if we would wish to find our way back to more measured and sensitive forms of architectural practice.

It is one of the paradoxes of the present that while the fashionable seem to be ever poised on the brink of a precipitous descent into self-indulgent artistry, the general level of architectural production grows more delicate and differentiated. From a global point of view one may claim that contemporary architecture has never been more vital even if this rigour is largely displayed in marginal, moderately scaled works, dispersed throughout the world. Today one will find the superior housing schemes in Delhi or Puchenau rather than in Paris or London or the finest stadia in Barcelona or Tokyo rather than in Munich or Los Angeles. As one might expect, such work tends to be removed from the current modernist versus historicist debate: the *reductio ad absurdum* of neo-avant-garde versus neo-nostalgic. Between these equally demagogic alternatives there still remains the possibility of continuing with the century-old tradition of modernity and the significance of the Patkau practice lies in its critical cultivation of this tradition at its best.

Appendices

Patkau Architects was founded by John and Patricia Patkau in Edmonton, Alberta in 1978. In 1984, the firm was relocated to Vancouver, British Columbia. Michael Cunningham became an associate in 1993.

John Patkau studied at the University of Manitoba, receiving a Bachelor of Arts and a Bachelor of Environmental Studies in 1969, and a Master of Architecture in 1972. Upon graduation he received the Royal Architectural Institute of Canada Medal. He is a fellow of the Royal Architectural Institute of Canada.

Patricia Patkau studied at the University of Manitoba, receiving a Bachelor of Interior Design degree in 1973. Upon graduation, she received the University of Manitoba Gold Medal. Following this, she studied at Yale University receiving a Master of Architecture in 1978. She is a fellow of the Royal Architectural Institute of Canada.

In addition to practice, Patricia was a member of the Faculty of Architecture at the University of California at Los Angeles from 1988 to 1990. She is presently an Associate Professor at the School of Architecture at the University of British Columbia in Vancouver.

Michael Cunningham studied at the University of Calgary, receiving a Bachelor of Arts in 1977 and a Master of Environmental Design (Architecture) in 1982. Upon graduation he received the Royal Architectural Institute of Canada Medal.

Strawberry Vale Elementary School
Victoria, British Columbia, 1992-1995
Client: Greater Victoria School District.
Architect: Patkau Architects.
Project Team: Grace Cheung, Michael
Cunningham, Michael Kothke, Tim Newton,
John Patkau, Patricia Patkau, David Shone,
Peter Suter, Jacqueline Wang.
Consultants: C.Y. Loh Associates Ltd.,
structural, D.W. Thomson Consultants Ltd.,
mechanical, Reid Crowther & Partners Ltd.,
electrical, Moura Quayle/Lanarc Consultants
Ltd., landscape, Gage Babcock & Associates,
fire protection, B.T.Y. Group, costing, Barron
Kennedy Lyzun & Associates, acoustics.

Charles Scott Gallery Renovation
Vancouver, British Columbia, 1992-1993
Client: Emily Carr College of Art and Design.
Architect: Patkau Architects in joint venture
with Toby Russell Buckwell & Partners.
Project Team: John Patkau, Patricia Patkau,
David Shone, Allan Teramura.
Consultants: Choukalos Woodburn McKenzie
Maranda Ltd., structural, Reid Crowther &
Partners Ltd., mechanical and electrical, B.T.Y.
Group, costing, Gabriel / design, lighting,
General Contractor: CDC Construction.

Barnes House
Nanaimo, British Columbia, 1991-1993
Client: David and Fran Barnes.
Architect: Patkau Architects
Project Team: Tim Newton, John Patkau,
Patricia Patkau, David Shone, Tom Robertson.
Consultants: Fast & Epp Partners, structural.
General Contractor: R.W. (Bob) Wall Ltd.

Emily Carr College of Art and Design
Vancouver, British Columbia, 1991-1994
Client: Emily Carr College of Art and Design.
Architect: Patkau Architects in joint venture
with Toby Russell Buckwell & Partners.
Project Team: Brad Cameron, Michael
Cunningham, Tim Newton, John Patkau,
Patricia Patkau, Tom Robertson, David Shone,
Barry Stanton, Allan Teramura.
Consultants: Choukalos Woodburn McKenzie
Maranda Ltd., structural, Reid Crowther &
Partners Ltd., mechanical and electrical, B.T.Y.
Group, costing, Gabriel / design, lighting,
Brown Strachan Associates, acoustics, Gage
Babcock & Associates, code and fire protection.
General Contractor: Granwest Constructors.

Peacekeeping Monument Competition
Ottawa, Ontario, 1990
Sponsor: National Capital Commission.
Architect: Patkau Architects with Roland
Brener, sculptor.
Project Team: Tony Griffin, John Patkau,
Patricia Patkau.

Newton Seniors Centre
Surrey, British Columbia, 1990-1992
Client: Corporation of the District of Surrey.
Architect: Patkau Architects
Project Team: Michael Cunningham, John
Patkau, Patricia Patkau, David Shone,
Peter Suter.
Consultants: C.Y. Loh Associates Ltd.,
structural, D.W. Thomson Consultants Ltd.,
mechanical, R.A. Duff & Associates Inc.,
electrical, B.T.Y. Group, costing, Brown
Strachan Associates, acoustics.
General Contractor: Nova Construction Ltd.

Newton Library
Surrey, British Columbia, 1990-1992
Client: Corporation of the District of Surrey.
Architect: Patkau Architects.
Project Team: Michael Cunningham, John
Patkau, Patricia Patkau, David Shone, Peter
Suter. Model maker, Peter Wood.
Consultants: C.Y. Loh Associates Ltd.,
structural, D.W. Thomson Consultants Ltd.,
mechanical, R.A. Duff & Associates Inc.,
electrical, B.T.Y. Group, costing, Brown
Strachan Associates, acoustics.
General Contractor: Farmer Construction Ltd.

Potuzak House
West Vancouver, British Columbia, 1989
Client: Christine and Rob Potuzak.
Architect: Patkau Architects.
Project Team: John Patkau, Patricia Patkau,
Elizabeth Shotton, Peter Suter.
Consultants: Smith & Company, structural,
Moura Quayle, landscape.

Canadian Clay and Glass Gallery
Waterloo, Ontario, 1988-1992
Client: Canadian Clay and Glass Gallery.
Architect: Patkau Architects with Mark
Musselman McIntyre Combe Inc. associate
architect.
Project Team: Michael Cunningham, Tony
Griffin, John Patkau, Patricia Patkau,
Peter Suter.
Consultants: C.Y. Loh Associates Ltd.,
structural, Keen Engineering Co. Ltd., Gabriel
Design / Lighting; mechanical, R.A. Duff
Company Ltd., electrical, Hanscomb
Consultants Inc., costing.
General Contractor: Ball Brothers Ltd.

Seabird Island School
Agassiz, British Columbia, 1988-1991
Client: Seabird Island Band.
Architect: Patkau Architects.
Project Team: Greg Johnson, John Patkau,
Patricia Patkau, Elizabeth Shotton, Tom Van
Driel, Model maker, Gina Dhein.

Consultants: C.Y. Loh Associates Ltd.,
structural, D.W. Thomson Consultants Ltd.,
mechanical and electrical, Hanscomb
Consultants Inc., costing, Christopher Phillips &
Associates, landscape, Novatec Consultants
Inc., site development.
Contract managers: Newhaven Projects Ltd.

Ma House
Vancouver, British Columbia, 1988-1989
Client: Wing Man Ma.
Architect: Patkau Architects.
Project Team: John Patkau, Patricia Patkau.
Consultants: C.Y. Loh Associates Ltd.,
structural.
General Contractor: Terry Gamel / G.R.
Construction Ltd.

Greene House
West Vancouver, British Columbia, 1987-1988
Client: Charles and Sheila Greene.
Architect: Patkau Architects.
Project Team: Shelly Craig, Greg Johnson, John
Patkau, Patricia Patkau.
Consultants: C.Y. Loh Associates Ltd.,
structural, Cornerlia Hahn Oberlander,
landscape.
General Contractor: G.R. Construction Ltd.

Kustin House
Los Angeles, California, 1986
Client: Barry and Frankie Kustin.
Architect: Patkau Architects.
Project Team: Shelly Craig, Greg Johnson, John
Patkau, Patricia Patkau, Chris Rowe.
Consultants: C.Y. Loh Associates Ltd.

Canadian Clay and Glass Gallery Competition
Waterloo, Ontario, 1986
Sponsor: Canadian Clay and Glass Gallery.
Architect: Patkau Architects.
Project Team: Shelly Craig, John Patkau,
Patricia Patkau, Chris Rowe.
Consultants: C.Y. Loh Associates Ltd.,
structural.

McCutcheon House
Vancouver, British Columbia, 1986
Client: Ross McCutcheon.
Architect: Patkau Architects.
Project Team: Shelly Craig, John Patkau,
Patricia Patkau, Mark Vaughn.
Consultants: C.Y. Loh Associates Ltd.,
structural.

Appleton House
Victoria, British Columbia, 1985-1986
Client: Doreen and Ian Appleton.
Architect: Patkau Architects.
Project Team: Greg Johnson, John Patkau,
Patricia Patkau. Model maker, Martin
Davidson.
Consultants: C.Y. Loh Associates Ltd, structural.
General Contractor: Doreen Appleton.

Porter/Vandenbosch Renovation
Toronto, Ontario, 1985-1986
Client: Gerald Porter and Betty Vandenbosch
Architect: Patkau Architects.
Project Team: John Patkau, Patricia Patkau
Consultants: C.Y. Loh Associates Ltd.,
structural.
General Contractor: Porter/Sheady
Construction.

Fountains Competition
Vieux-Port de Montreal
Montreal, Quebec, 1984
Sponsor: City of Montreal.
Architect: Patkau Architects.
Project Team: Daryl Favor, John Patkau, Patricia
Patkau, Gordon Robinson, Tom Zimmerman.

Patkau House
West Vancouver, British Columbia, 1984-1985
Client: John and Patricia Patkau.
Architect: Patkau Architects.
Project Team: John Patkau, Patricia Patkau
Consultants: C.Y. Loh Associates Ltd.,
structural.
General Contractor: Calrudd Construction Ltd.

Apartment Renovation
Toronto, Ontario, 1984
Client: Karen Patkau.
Architect: Patkau Architects.
Project Team: John Patkau, Patricia Patkau.
General Contractor: Colin Lochhead.

Pyrch House
Victoria, British Columbia, 1983-1984
Client: Al and Mary-Ellen Pyrch.
Architect: Patkau Architects.
Project Team: John Patkau, Patricia Patkau,
Tom Van Driel, Jacqueline Wang.
Consultants: Halsall Stanley Associates Ltd.,
structural, Cornerlia Hahn Oberlander,
landscape.
General Contractor: Madrona Bay Homes Ltd.

Research Office,
Alberta Research Council
Edmonton, Alberta, 1982
Client: Alberta Housing and Public Works.
Architect: Patkau Architects.
Project Team: John Patkau, Patricia Patkau,
Jacqueline Wang.

Blue Quill School
Edmonton, Alberta, 1982
Client: Edmonton Public Schools.
Architect: Patkau Architects.
Project Team: John Patkau, Patricia Patkau,
Tom Van Driel, Jacqueline Wang.
Consultants: Halsall Stanley Associates Ltd.,
structural, Cheriton Engineering Ltd.,
mechanical, A.M.E. Engineering Ltd., electrical,
Lombard North Group (1980) Ltd., landscape,
Hanscomb Consultants Inc., costing.

Driver Examination Office
Grande Prairie, Alberta, 1981-1983
Client: Alberta Housing and Public Works.
Architect: Patkau Architects.
Project Team: John Patkau, Patricia Patkau,
Tom Van Driel.
Consultants: Halsall Stanley Associates Ltd.,
structural, Cheriton Engineering Ltd.,
mechanical, Putters Banani & Associates Ltd.,
electrical, MTB Consultants, landscape.
General Contractor: Dan's Construction
(1977) Ltd.

Driver Examination Office
Fort McMurray, Alberta, 1981-1983
Client: Alberta Housing and Public Works.
Architect: Patkau Architects.
Project Team: John Patkau, Patricia Patkau,
Tom Van Driel.
Consultants: Halsall Stanley Associates Ltd.,
structural, Cheriton Engineering Ltd.,
mechanical, Putters Banani & Associates Ltd.,
electrical, MTB Consultants, landscape.
General Contractor: L.C. Greenough
Construction Ltd.

Fournier House
Edmonton, Alberta, 1981
Client: Bob and Millie Fournier.
Architect: Patkau Architects.
Project Team: John Patkau, Patricia Patkau,
Tom Van Driel.

Edmonton City Hall Competition
Edmonton, Alberta, 1980
Sponsor: City of Edmonton.
Architect: Patkau Architects.
Project Team: John Patkau, Patricia Patkau.

Riverdale Community Centre
Edmonton, Alberta, 1980-1981
Client: City of Edmonton.
Architect: Patkau Architects in joint venture
with Norbert Lemermeyer Architect Ltd.
Project Team: John Patkau, Patricia Patkau.
Consultants: MB Engineering, structural, Gilbert
M. Rekken & Associates Ltd., mechanical, Jarvis
Engineering Ltd.,
electrical.

Alexander Garden
Edmonton, Alberta, 1980
Client: Keith and Vanessa Alexander.
Architect: Patkau Architects.
Project Team: John Patkau, Patricia Patkau.

McGregor House
Edmonton, Alberta, 1979-1982
Client: Barbara and Stewart McGregor.
Architect: Patkau Architects.
Project Team: John Patkau, Patricia Patkau,
Tom Van Driel.
Consultants: Duthie Newby & Associates Ltd.,
structural.
General Contractor: Ed Lusis.

Haynes Studio
Edmonton, Alberta, 1979
Client: Doug Haynes.
Architect: Patkau Architects.
Project Team: John Patkau, Patricia Patkau.

Galleria Condominium
Edmonton, Alberta, 1978-1981
Client: E.S.I. Holdings Ltd.
Architect: Patkau Architects.
Project Team: John Patkau, Patricia Patkau,
Tom Van Driel.
Consultants: MB Engineering Ltd., structural,
Vinto Engineering Ltd., mechanical, Allsopp
Morgan Engineering Ltd., electrical, MTB
Consultants Ltd., landscape.
General Contractor: Builder's Contract
Management Ltd.

Awards

1993
Progressive Architecture Award
Barnes House

1992
Canadian Architect Award of Excellence
Barnes House

1992
Governor General's Medal for Architecture
Seabird Island School

1992
Lieutenant Governor's Medal for Architecture
Seabird Island School

1992
Canadian Wood Council Honour Award
Seabird Island School

1990
Canadian Architect Award of Excellence
Canadian Clay and Glass Gallery

1990
Governor General's Medal for Architecture
Appleton Residence

1990
Governor General's Award for Architecture
Porter/Vandenbosch Residence

1989
Canadian Architect Award of Excellence
Seabird Island School

1988
Architectural Institute of British
Columbia Honour Award
Pyrch Residence

1987
Canadian Architect Award of Excellence
Kustin Residence

1986
Winning Submission
Canadian Clay and Glass
Gallery Competition

1986
Canadian Architect Award of Excellence
Appleton Residence

1986
Governor General's Medal for Architecture
Pyrch Residence

1984
Canadian Architect Award of Excellence
Research Office, ARC

1984
Canadian Architect Award of Excellence
Pyrch Residence

1984
Canadian Wood Council First Award
McGregor Residence

1983
Canadian Architect Award of Excellence
Blue Quill School

1981
Progressive Architecture Citation
Galleria Condominium

Exhibitions

1994
Travelling European Exhibition
London, RIBA Gallery; Edinburgh, Matthew
Architecture Gallery; Barcelona, CAC Sala
Picasso

1993
International Architectural Exhibition and Sale
Southern California Institute of Architecture
Los Angeles, California

1992
The Lieutenant Governors Medals for
Architecture
Architectural Institute of British Columbia
Vancouver, British Columbia

1992
Patkau Architects: Recent Projects
William McCarley's Books
Vancouver, British Columbia

1991
Architecture in Perspective
Inform Interiors
Vancouver, British Columbia

1991
Spaces & Spirits Exhibition
Vancouver Trade and Convention Centre
Vancouver, British Columbia

1991
Patkau Architects: Recent Projects
Ballenford Architectural Books
Toronto, Ontario

1990
Patkau Architects: Projects 1978-1990
University of British Columbia Fine Arts Gallery
Vancouver, British Columbia

1988
National travelling exhibition of the firm's work
Sponsored by the University of Toronto
Toronto, Ontario

1988
The University of Manitoba Alumni Show
Winnipeg Art Gallery
Winnipeg, Manitoba

1987
Entries for the Canadian Clay and Glass Gallery
Architectural Competition
The University of British Columbia Fine Arts
Gallery, Vancouver, British Columbia;
Seagram Museum Waterloo, Ontario

1986
Governor General's Medals for Architecture
Robson Media Centre
Vancouver, British Columbia

1986
The House Revisited
Inform Interiors
Vancouver, British Columbia

1986
A Measure of Consensus: Canadian
Architecture in Transition
The University of British Columbia Fine Arts
Gallery, Vancouver, British Columbia;
49th Parallel New York, New York;
Harbourfront Gallery Toronto, Ontario.

1986
Architects' Drawings
Charles A. Scott Gallery, Emily Carr College of
Art and Design, Vancouver, British Columbia

1983
The Design Workshop
Edmonton, Alberta

1982
Ten Schools
Edmonton, Alberta

1982
International Music and Architecture Festival
Aguila, Italy

1993

Kenneth Frampton. 'John and Patricia Patkau' in "America Incognito: An Anthology." Casabella LVII: 607 (December 1993) p. 51, pp. 62-63. Seabird Island School, Agassiz, British Columbia.

Connie HItzeroth. "Clay & Glass Gallery enhances art it displays." *The Financial Post,* September 18, 1993. Canadian Clay and Glass Gallery, Waterloo, Ontario.

Chrisopher Hume. "Design sparkles like crystal at gallery for clay and glass." *The Toronto Star,* June 9, 1993. Canadian Clay and Glass Gallery, Waterloo, Ontario.

John and Patricia Patkau, In Canadian Clay and Glass Gallery, Vision to Reality, 1981-93. (Waterloo: Canadian Clay and Glass Gallery, 1993), Exhibition Catalogue, p.4

John Patkau with Anne McPherson. "Victory at Waterloo (interview)." Ontario Craft XVIII: 2 (Summer 1993). p. 8-12. Canadian Clay and Glass Gallery, Waterloo, Ontario.

Adele Freedman. "A space to get fired up about." *The Globe and Mail,* June 19, 1993. Canadian Clay and Glass Gallery, Waterloo Ontario.

Rhys Phillips. "Waterloo gallery a triumph of architecture." *The Ottawa Citizen,* May 29, 1993. Canadian Clay and Glass Gallery, Waterloo, Ontario.

Annette Le Cuyer "Engaging Extrovert." *Architectural Review* (May 1993) p.16-19. Newton Library, Surrey, British Columbia.

Brian Carter. "Cultural Precinct". *Architectural Review* (May 1993) p.20-23. Canadian Clay and Glass Gallery, Waterloo, Ontario.

Annette Le Cuyer. "Native Wit". *Architectural Review* (May 1993) p.47-49.

Catherine Slessor. "Modern Metamorphosis". *Architectural Review* (May 1993) p.86-87. Porter / Vandenbosch House, Toronto, Ontario.

Brian Carter. "Civic Exuberance: Newton Library" *The Canadian Architect* XXXVIII: 5 (May, 1993) p. 16-21. Newton Library, Surrey, British Columbia. Interview with John Patkau, p. 22-28.

Rhys Phillips. "B.C. home architecture 'continuous with natural world'." *The Ottawa Citizen,* February 20, 1993. Barnes House, Nanaimo, British Columbia.

"Architectural Design Award: Patkau Architects." *Progressive Architecture* LXXIV: 1 (January, 1993, "40th Annual P/A Awards") p. 50-53. Barnes House, Nanaimo, British Columbia.

1992

Brian Carter, ed. *The Canadian Clay and Glass Gallery: The Act of Transformation.* (Halifax: Technical University of Nova Scotia Resource Centre Publications, 1992.) p. 37-47, p. 119-143.

"Seabird Island School: Patkau Architects Inc." The Governor General's Awards for Architecture 1992, The Royal Architectural Institute of Canada, p. 58-63.

"Award of Excellence: Barnes House, Nanaimo, B.C., Patkau Architects" *The Canadian Architect* XXXVII: 12 (December 1992, "1992 Awards of Excellence") p. 20-21.

"Ancestral Forms." *The Architectural Review,* Volume CXCI, No. 1148, (October, 1992) p. 43-45. Seabird Island School, Agassiz, British Columbia.

Sandra McKenzie. "John and Patricia Patkau." *Canadian House and Home.* XIV:3 (May/June, 1992) p. 62-67, 87. Appleton House, Victoria, British Columbia, Porter/Vandenbosch House, Toronto, Ontario.

Donald Canty. "Aerodynamic School." *Progressive Architecture* (May 1992) p.142-147. Seabird Island School, Agassiz, British Columbia.

Adele Freedman. "Of 'birdness' and 'bugness' and a fresh, complex vision." *The Globe and Mail,* March 7, 1992. Newton Library, Surrey, British Columbia.

Andrew Gruft. "Seabird Island Community School." *The Canadian Architect* XXXVII:1 (January, 1992) p.14-23.

Catherine Ormell. "Is it a fish? Is it a bird? Yes, and it's an ark of learning." *The Independent,* January 15, 1992. Seabird Island School, Agassiz, British Columbia.

1991
"Engineering Nature." *Architecture* (September, 1991) p. 100. Seabird Island School, Agassiz, British Columbia.

Trevor Boddy. "Pacific Patkau." *The Architectural Review,* Volume CLXXXIX No. 1134, (August 1991) p. 32-38. Pyrch House, Victoria, British Columbia, Seabird Island School, Agassiz, British Columbia, Kustin House, Los Angeles, California.

Christopher Hume. "Building in the Natural World: West Coast architects' designs blend with their surroundings." *The Toronto Star,* March 9, 1991.

1990
Adele Freedman, "John and Patricia Patkau." In: Sight Lines: *Looking at Architecture and Design in Canada* (Don Mills, Ontario: Oxford University Press, 1990) p. 88-91

Andrew Gruft, "Notes on the Architecture of John and Patricia Patkau." In: *Patkau Architects: Projects 1978-1990,* (Vancouver: UBC Fine Arts Gallery, 1990) Exhibition catalogue.

Clare Lorenz. "Patricia Patkau." In: *Women in Architecture: A Contemporary View,* (New York: Rizzoli International Publications Inc, 1990) p. 92-95

"Award of Excellence: Canadian Clay and Glass Gallery, Waterloo, Ontario, Patkau Architects." *The Canadian Architect* XXXV: 12 (December 1990, "1990 Awards of Excellence"), p. 20-21.

Odile Henault. "Vancouver: Patricia et John Patkau." *L'Architecture d'Aujourd'hui* no. 270, (September 1990), p. 148-162. Porter/Vandenbosch House, Toronto, Ontario, Kustin House, Los Angeles, California, Greene House, West Vancouver, British Columbia, Appleton House, Victoria, British Columbia.

"Selected Details: Rumford Fireplace, Appleton Residence, Victoria, British Columbia." *Progressive Architecture* LXXI: 1 (January 1990), p. 175.

Christian W. Thomsen. "Mit Volldampf zurück in die Zukunft / Full Steam Backwards into Modernism," Häuser, 1990, no.2, p. 142-147, unpaginated English summary at front of issue. Greene House, West Vancouver, British Columbia.

Christian W. Thomsen, "Architektur pur in Harmonie mit der Natur / In Harmony with Nature," Häuser, 1990, no. 1, p. 38-44, unpaginated English summary in front of issue. Patkau House, West Vancouver, British Columbia.

"Appleton Residence, Patkau Architects" In: Governor General's Awards for Architecture 1990, The Royal Architectural Institute of Canada, p. 34-39

"Porter/Vandenbosch Residence, Patkau Architects," In: Governor General's Awards for Architecture 1990, The Royal Architectural Institute of Canada, p. 948-101.

1989
"Award of Excellence: Seabird Island School, Agassiz, B.C., Patkau Architects." *The Canadian Architect* XXXIV: 12 (December 1989, "1989 Awards of Excellence"), p. 25-27.

1988

Ruth Cawker and William Bernstein. "The Pyrch Residence." In: *Contemporary Canadian Architecture: The Mainstream and Beyond.* (Markham, Ont.: Fitzhenry & Whiteside Ltd., 1988), p. 206-208.

1987

Trevor Boddy. "The Bush League: Four Approaches to Regionalism in Recent Canadian Architecture." In: *Centre: a Journal for Architecture in America* III (1987), p. 100-107.

"Award of Excellence: Kustin Residence, Los Angeles, Patkau Architects." *The Canadian Architect* XXXII: 12 (December 1987), p. 32-35

Stephen Godfrey. "Form & Function: Erickson's Heirs." *V Magazine* (Vancouver), September 1987, p. 84-85, 119.

1986

"Pyrch Residence. Architects: Patkau Associates / Architecture & Interior Design." In: 1986 Awards Program, Governor General's Medals for Architecture, (Ottawa: Royal Architectural Institute of Canada, 1986). p.19-22.

Martin Davidson and Frances Schmitt. "Blue Quill School, Edmonton, Alberta, 1982; Patkau Architects." In: Andrew Gruft, *A Measure of Consensus: Canadian Architecture in Transition.* (Vancouver: UBC Fine Arts Gallery, 1986), p. 11.

Andrew Gruft, "Analysis." In: *A Measure of Consensus,* p. 29-51.

"Award of Excellence: Appleton Residence, Victoria, B.C., Patkau Architects." *The Canadian Architect* XXXI: 12 (December 1986, "1986 Awards of Excellence"), p. 33-35.

Dennis Fitzgerald. "Site Specific." *Western Living* XVI (November 1986), p. 44j-44q. Pyrch House, Victoria, British Columbia.

Charles de Rudder. Cimaise sur l'Océan / Picture Gallery to the Ocean." *Vogue Decoration* 1986, no. 6 (June), p. 104-111. English summary.

John Patkau. "Northern Prairie House, Formal Order and Careful Detailing in a Large Home for a Family of Four." *Fine Homebuilding* no. 32 (April/May 1986), p. 24-28. McGregor House, Edmonton, Alberta.

"Elemental Gestures: Pyrch Residence, Victoria, B.C., Patkau Architects, Inc." *The Canadian Architect* XXXI: 1 (January 1986), p.12-15.

1985

Architects Drawings. (Vancouver: The Charles H. Scott Gallery, Emily Carr College of Art and Design, 1985.) Exhibition catalogue.

1984

"Award of Excellence: Patkau Architects, Pyrch Residence, Victoria, B.C." *The Canadian Architect* XXIX: 12 (December 1984, "The 1984 Annual Awards of Excellence'), p. 18-21.

"Award of Excellence: Patkau Architects, Research Office, Alberta Research Council, Edmonton." *The Canadian Architect* XXIX: 12 (December 1984, "The 1984 Annual Awards of Excellence"), p. 40-42.

Peter Hemingway. "Exercise in Nostalgia: Private Residence, Edmonton; Architect, Patkau Architects." *The Canadian Architect* XXIX: 5 (May 1984), p. 22-26.

1983

"Architect: Patkau Architects; Award of Excellence: Blue Quill School, Edmonton." *The Canadian Architect* XXVII: 12 (December 1983, "The 1983 Canadian Architect Awards of Excellence"), p. 20-23.

1981

"Architectural Design Citation: John and Patricia Patkau, John Patkau Architect." *Progressive Architecture* LXII: 1, (January 1981, "The 28th P/A Awards"). p. 142-143. Residential condominium, Edmonton, Alberta.

Photography credits

James Dow
12, 14, 22, 23, 24, 25, 26, 27, 31 upper, 40, 41, 43, 44, 45, 50, 53, 54, 55, 56, 57, 58, 62, 63, 64 upper, 65, 66, 67, 68, 69, 84, 85, 86, 89, 90, 91, 92, 93, 94, 97, 98, 103, 105.

Steven Evans
33, 35, 37, 38, 39, 70, 76, 77 upper, 80 lower.

William E Nassau
74.

Patkau Architects
11, 29, 31 lower, 33, 51, 60, 64 lower, 71, 72, 75, 78, 79, 80 upper, 81, 82, 83, 100, 101, 102, 104.

Gerald Porter
35.

Provincial Archives of Manitoba
Hudson's Bay Company Archives
8.

Royal British Columbia Museum
C.F. Newcombe
15.

Norm Spanos
77 lower.

Horst Thanhäuser
28, 30, 32.

Essy Baniassad is an architect who has been active both in practice and as an educator. He is the Dean of Architecture at the Technical University of Nova Scotia and a past president of the Royal Architectural Institute of Canada.

Brian Carter is an architect working in practice in London, England. His architectural criticism has been published in a series of books and international journals. He is a Visiting Professor at the Technical University of Nova Scotia.

Kenneth Frampton is Ware Professor of Architecture at Columbia University. He is an architect and architectural historian.

Beth Kapusta is a graduate of the School of Architecture at the University of Waterloo and is the assistant editor of *The Canadian Architect*.

Bronwen Ledger is the editor of *The Canadian Architect* and is based in Toronto.

Marco Polo is an architect working in practice in Toronto. His writings on architecture have been published in a number of journals.